The Secret Power of

GRACE

THE BOOK OF 1 PETER

Other books in the growing Faithgirlz!™ library

Bibles
The Faithgirlz! Bible
NIV Faithgirlz! Backpack Bible

Bible Studies
Secret Power of Love
Secret Power of Joy
Secret Power of Goodness
Secret Power of Grace

Nonfiction
Faithgirlz Journal
The Faithgirlz! Handbook
Food, Faith and Fun: The Faithgirlz! Cookbook
No Boys Allowed
What's A Girl To Do?
Girlz Rock
Chick Chat
Real Girls of the Bible
Faithgirlz! Whatever
My Beautiful Daughter
Beauty Lab
Body Talk
Everybody Tells Me to Be Myself, But I Don't Know Who I Am
Girl Politics

Fiction

From Sadie's Sketchbook
Shades of Truth (Book One)
Flickering Hope (Book Two)
Waves of Light (Book Three)
Brilliant Hues (Book Four)

Boarding School Mysteries
Vanished (Book One)
Betrayed (Book Two)
Burned (Book Three)
Poisoned (Book Four)

Sophie's World
Sophie's World
Sophie's Secret
Sophie Under Pressure
Sophie Steps Up
Sophie's First Dance
Sophie's Stormy Summer
Sophie's Friendship Fiasco
Sophie and the New Girl
Sophie Flakes Out
Sophie Loves Jimmy
Sophie's Drama
Sophie Gets Real

The Girls of Harbor View
Girl Power
Take Charge
Raising Faith
Secret Admirer

The Lucy Series
Lucy Doesn't Wear Pink (Book One)
Lucy Out of Bounds (Book Two)
Lucy's Perfect Summer (Book Three)
Lucy Finds Her Way (Book Four)

Check out www.faithgirlz.com

faiThGirLz!
BIBLE STUDY

The Secret Power of
GRACE

THE BOOK OF 1 PETER

Susie Shellenberger

ZONDERVAN®

ZONDERVAN.com/
AUTHORTRACKER
follow your favorite authors

ZONDERKIDZ

The Secret Power of Grace
Copyright © 2012 by Susie Shellenberger

Illustrations © 2012 by Zonderkidz

This title is also available as a Zondervan ebook.
Visit www.zondervan.com/ebooks

Requests for information should be addressed to:
Zonderkidz, 5300 Patterson Ave. SE, Grand Rapids, Michigan 49530

ISBN 978-0310-72840-5

Published in association with the literary agency of Alive Communica-
tions, Inc., 7680 Goddard Street, Suite 200, Colorado Springs, CO 80920.
www.alivecommunications.com

Zonderkidz is a trademark of Zondervan.

Editor: Kim Childress
Cover design: Kris Nelson
Interior design: Sarah Molegraaf

Printed in the United States of America

12 13 14 15 16 17 18 19 /DCI/ 19 18 17 16 15 14 13 12 11 10 9 8 7 6 5 4 3 2 1

Dedicated to
Stephane Shellenberger.
Thank you for being the sister I never had.

Table of Contents

Introduction

Read this first!

Adrienne was in tears by the time she got home. She grabbed her purple gel pen and her journal and scribbled her thoughts on the lines.

> I'm so tired of those guys making fun of me. It's not fair! I'm a good person. I don't deserve to be hassled all the time. It all started when Derek found out I go to church. He's been making fun of me ever since. I've had enough! I feel like such a loser. And I totally hate the way I look! I'm such a geek. I wish I were beautiful like Jenna. Tomorrow I'll get even with Derek. I'm gonna spread some rumors about him that will make him sorry he ever met me! I'm gonna text everyone I know, and I'm gonna post stuff about him on Facebook. I'll show him!

Meredith walked home shifting her backpack from side to side adjusting the weight of her books and homework.

What a day, she thought. *Alan tripped me again and made fun of my faith. Troy knocked my books out of my locker and made fun of my Bible because I wouldn't laugh at his stupid jokes. Aimee totally lied about me to Mrs. Phillips, and now I'm not allowed to try out for the school play!* Can it get any worse?

Meredith reviewed the day in her mind. *I'm so sick of Adam making fun of my hair. I can't help it that it's all curls.*

She shifted her backpack to her left arm.

"God," she began. "I've had a rotten day. I don't feel good about myself, but I'm choosing to like myself anyway. Curls and all!" Meredith loved walking home from school, because it gave her a chance to go through her day with God. People could be so cruel. But like Mom said, in five years, no one will care if I have curly hair.

"Yeah, I know I've blown it out of perspective. After all, my years in high school aren't eternity. They'll be over before I know it. And ten years from now, what will it matter that I didn't get a part in the school play, or that Troy knocked my books out of my locker?" And she thought about what Dad told her before when people made fun of her hair. "How do you think God sees you?" Tomorrow she might shake her curls next to Adam just for fun.

"God, I'm sorry I've been so self-absorbed today. Will

you forgive me? I'm so glad you love me no matter what! You make me feel like a winner!"

By the time Meredith reached her house, she had focused her thoughts on her homework and how she could reach out to the new girl in her geometry class.

Meredith knew a few secrets that Adrienne hadn't learned. Meredith was a Secret Power Girl! She thought about things from God's point of view, and it helped her feel better in every situation—even if it took a little while. She started to learn how God viewed the big picture.

Wanna know more?

Then dive into 1 Peter and discover these secrets for yourself!

This is Who You Really Are!

1 Peter 1:1-25

Where is it? In the New Testament, after James and before 2 Peter.

Who wrote it? Peter.

Who was he? Peter was a fisherman. You know that passage, fishers of men... He was the second disciple that Jesus chose when he selected the group of twelve. Andrew, Peter's younger brother, was the first disciple chosen by Christ, but Peter is always mentioned first when the disciples are listed by name. This is probably because he was a natural leader. He was outspoken and impulsive, and sometimes, he acted before he thought. But he had a tender heart and a willingness to be used by God.

We can identify with Peter's failures, and we gain encouragement from watching Christ turn his weaknesses into strengths. Jesus saw past Peter's weak areas and focused on his potential. Even though Peter was impatient and sometimes stubborn, Christ saw his potential as a *rock*—the future foundation of the Church.

Christ does the same with us. Instead of remembering our failures, he looks at our potential, our talents, and ways we can help do God's work.

BITE #1:

Peter, an apostle of Jesus Christ, to God's elect, exiles, scattered throughout the provinces of Pontus, Galatia, Cappadocia, Asia and Bithynia, who have been chosen according to the foreknowledge of God the Father, through the sanctifying work of the Spirit, to be obedient to Jesus Christ and sprinkled with his blood.

1 Peter 1:1-2

The book of 1 Peter begins with a salutation. A salutation is...

_____ a. something you put on a salad;

_____ b. a special salute that's used in today's military;

_____ c. a greeting; or

_____ d. a type of exercise in which a boxer engages.

If you selected "a greeting," you're right on the mark. Go back and read Peter's salutation again. What else does this greeting include? Mark all that apply.

_____ a. Christmas wishes.

_____ b. The identity of the writer.

_____ c. To whom the writer belongs.

_____ d. A recipe for chocolate chip cookies.

We can tell by Peter's salutation that he's **extremely clear** about his **identity**. He knows who he is and to whom he belongs. Do you ever wonder about your identity?

Though it may be hard to imagine or remember when you most need to, God created you. You were formed in **God's holy image**. So shouldn't it make sense that you can find your identity in God? The next time you're unsure of yourself or wonder who you really are, remember, **you are a child of God!**

The more you develop your relationship with Christ, the more secure you'll become in who you are. So stop right now and give yourself a standing ovation, because by participating in this Bible study, you're actually deepening your relationship with Jesus and getting to know him better. And that equals getting to know *you* better!

Peter identifies himself as an apostle. An apostle is...

_____ a. a fancy name for a Greek dish served with rice.

_____ b. a special buckle worn on sandals in Bible days.

_____ c. a special messenger of Jesus Christ.

_____ d. a history buff.

An apostle is not only a special **messenger** of Jesus Christ, but also someone who Jesus gave **authority** for certain tasks. The twelve disciples who Jesus first chose to follow him were also known as apostles. Sometimes throughout the New Testament, the word *apostle* is used in a general sense, meaning "God's messenger."

Grab your Bible and flip to 2 Corinthians 8:23.

> As for Titus, he is my partner and co-worker among you; as for our brothers, they are representatives of the churches and an honor to Christ.
>
> 2 Corinthians 8:23

In this verse, Paul describes people who have the responsibility of representing the church. He refers to them as apostles, messengers, or representatives, (depending on which translation of the Bible you're reading). Read the verse again.

Whom does Paul identify as his fellow worker in this particular passage?

_____ a. Titus

_____ b. Peter

_____ c. Samuel

_____ d. Matthew

As the first apostles planted churches and spread the news of Jesus Christ, they faced **threats** and danger. When persecution exploded, it was the apostles who were targeted. Grab your Bible again and turn to 1 Corinthians 4:9-13. According to this passage, how did the apostles respond to **persecution**?

Now turn to Romans 8:17-18. How did Paul view his suffering for Christ?

_____

_____

_____

_____

Before we get back to 1 Peter, let's take a quick peek at 2 Corinthians 1:5-7:

> For just as we share abundantly in the sufferings of Christ, so also our comfort abounds through Christ. If we are distressed, it is for your comfort and salvation; if we are comforted, it is for your comfort, which produces in you patient endurance of the same sufferings we suffer. And our hope for you is firm, because we know that just as you share in our sufferings, so also you share in our comfort.

Paul, an apostle of Christ, experienced suffering, yet what else did he experience on the positive side?

_____

_____

_____

_____

Describe a time in your life when you were picked on because of your faith.

_____

_____

_____

_____

_____

List other things that you've been given a hard time about. (Looks, clothes, hair, etc.)

_____

_____

_____

_____

_____

Do you realize that when God looks at you, he sees a princess? That's right! YOU are a princess of the King of Kings! When someone gives you a hard time because of your faith, your freckles, or your clothing, try to remember that YOU are God's princess.

Pretend you're tweeting. Tweet a one sentence prayer in the space provided, asking God to teach you how to experience comfort in the midst of your suffering.

_____

_____

_____

_____

_____

_____

_____

BITE #2

Peter, an apostle of Jesus Christ, to God's elect, exiles, scattered throughout the provinces of Pontus, Galatia, Cappadocia, Asia and Bithynia, who have been chosen according to the foreknowledge of God the Father, through the sanctifying work of the Spirit, to be obedient to Jesus Christ and sprinkled with his blood.

1 Peter 1:1-2

Peter is sure of his **identity** in Christ. He spells it out right up front. It's as if he's saying, "This is who I am! I'm sure of my calling from God, and I know who I am in Christ Jesus."

God wants **you** to be just as confident as Peter was. Rate yourself on the following scale to see where you score on knowing your place in Christ.

1. I'm curious about Jesus and want to know him better. I don't really understand who I am, but I'm hoping as I get to know God better, I'll become more secure in the God who created me.

2. I know Jesus as my personal Savior. I've asked him to forgive my sins, but my relationship with Jesus isn't really that strong. Sometimes, I doubt my faith, and I have a lot of questions about who I am.

3. I believe Jesus is my Savior, and I'm involved in church. But I can't say I'm really growing stronger in faith every day. I know I belong to God, and I

don't doubt God's with me, but things need to come together for me spiritually.

4. Like Peter, I know God has a special calling on my life. I'm not sure what it is yet—but that's okay, because I trust God. I still doubt myself, and I'm not sure how I fit into God's plan. I don't see how it all connects yet.

5. I am confident of my relationship with Christ. I believe his hand is on my life for a special purpose. I know he wants to use me to bring glory to God. I'm beginning to recognize the gifts and abilities God has blessed me with and am starting to use them for good. I don't have all the answers, but as I spend more time with God on a consistent basis, I find myself falling more and more in love with Jesus and growing closer to him. That makes me feel more and more complete and secure each day.

Peter, an apostle of Jesus Christ, to God's elect, exiles, scattered throughout the provinces of Pontus, Galatia, Cappadocia, Asia and Bithynia, who have been chosen according to the foreknowledge of God the Father, through the sanctifying work of the Spirit, to be obedient to Jesus Christ and sprinkled with his blood.

1 Peter 1:1-2

Faith-O-Meter

| 1 | 2 | 3 | 4 | 5 |

Peter refers to God's elect (the Christians) as strangers.
Why do you suppose he labels us this way?

_____ a. Because all Christians are weird.

_____ b. Because Christians wear funny clothes.

_____ c. Because Christians are aliens living in a world that's not their real home.

_____ d. Because Christians smell different.

As a Christian, your real home is in heaven. That means you're simply a traveler passing through planet earth. Don't get too attached to things here, because the bulk of your time won't be spent here. Think in terms of eternity—**forever**—which is how long you'll live in your real home, heaven!

When you view your life as an alien, or a stranger living in a world that's not your own, how does it change your perspective on the following?

Being persecuted for your faith.

_____

_____

_____

_____

Not wearing the most expensive and "in" clothing labels.

_____

_____

_____

_____

_____

Not always being included by popular students.

_____

_____

_____

_____

Experiencing rejection from friends or a boyfriend.

_____

_____

_____

_____

Grace and peace be yours in abundance.

-1 Peter 1:2

Grace-O-Meter

On a scale of 1 to 10 (1 being little and 10 being exceeding), how much grace and peace does God want you to have?

1   2   3   4   5   6   7   8   9   10

How much grace and peace are you actually experiencing?

1   2   3   4   5   6   7   8   9   10

If you're not experiencing as much grace and peace as God desires for you to have, why not?

_____

_____

_____

Praise be to the God and Father of our Lord Jesus Christ! In his great mercy, he has given us new birth into a living hope through the resurrection of Jesus Christ from the dead, and into an inheritance that can never perish, spoil or fade. This inheritance is kept in heaven for you.

1 Peter 1:3-4

Accepting Christ as your personal Savior is often referred to as being reborn. How is accepting Christ similar to a new birth? (Check out John 3:1-15 and 1 John 4:7).

_____

_____

_____

_____

_____

Peter states that you have an inheritance! How does that make you feel? (Check all that apply.)

_____ a. Rich

_____ b. Excited

_____ c. Curious

_____ d. Overwhelmed

As a Christian, what is your inheritance?

_____

_____

_____

Grab your Bible and flip over to Matthew 6:19-21. Where are we encouraged to place our treasures?

_____

_____

_____

What will happen to our treasures if we keep them on earth?

_____

_____

_____

List four material possessions that you treasure.

1. _____

2. _____

3. _____

4. _____

Which of the above would be the toughest to give up?

_____

_____

List four treasures you have that aren't material.

1. _____

2. _____

3. _____

4. _____

Which of the above would be the easiest to let go?

_____

_____

...who through faith are shielded by God's power until the coming of the salvation that is ready to be revealed in the last time.

1 Peter 1:5

In other words, God is going to make sure you get safely to heaven to receive the inheritance God has for you. Right now you are being **shielded** by God's power.

Should knowing this make a difference in how you live your daily life? If so, how?

_____

_____

_____

> In all this you greatly rejoice, though now for a little while you may have had to suffer grief in all kinds of trials.
>
> 1 Peter 1:6

Christians aren't exempt from hard times. Jesus never promised that we wouldn't have problems, but he **did** promise to help us through our problems.

Check this out:

> No temptation has overtaken you except what is common to mankind. And God is faithful; he will not let you be tempted beyond what you can bear. But when you are tempted, he will also provide a way out so that you can endure under it.
>
> 1 Corinthians 10:13

Mark the following statements true or false based on the above passage:

Sometimes your temptation will be so great, you'll simply have to give in.

_____ True   _____ False

Whenever you're tempted, you can take comfort in knowing you're not alone in this temptation. Someone, sometime, somewhere has also faced what you're struggling with.

_____ True   _____ False

Many areas of temptation are inescapable; there's no way out of the situation you face.

_____ True   _____ False

You will never be tempted beyond what you can bear with God's help.

_____ True   _____ False

Describe a temptation you have faced in the last week.

_____

_____

_____

_____

_____

How did you handle it? (Did you give in? Walk away? Pray? Talk with a friend?)

_____

_____

_____

_____

_____

What will you do the next time you face the same temptation?

_____

_____

_____

_____

_____

These have come so that the proven genuineness of your faith—of greater worth than gold, which perishes even though refined by fire—may result in praise, glory and honor when Jesus Christ is revealed.

1 Peter 1:7

What good does the above Scripture promise will come from our trials?

_____

_____

_____

_____

Think back to your most recent trial. How was (or how could) God's name be praised because of what you

experienced? How did you bring God glory? (Or how could you have brought God glory?)

_____

_____

_____

_____

_____

Your faith is invaluable! In fact, Peter says it's worth more than...

_____ a. silver.

_____ b. bronze.

_____ c. gold.

_____ d. diamonds.

Fire purifies gold. Describe how trials and suffering for Christ refines or purifies your faith.

_____

_____

_____

_____

_____

When you're hit with a trial, you probably don't think, *Great! Now's my chance to become refined.* You might not understand how your trials can be used for God's purpose. Maybe if you experience people making fun of you, you might then help someone else. But **know** that God has your best interests at heart—and that Christ can be glorified through **all** your trials.

Write a prayer to God in the space provided asking for God's Spirit to help you view your tough times in a different light.

_____

_____

_____

_____

_____

_____

BITE #3

> Though you have not seen him, you love him; and even
> though you do not see him now, you believe in him and
> are filled with an inexpressible and glorious joy, for you
> are receiving the end result of your faith, the salvation of
> your souls.
>
> 1 Peter 1:8-9

Notice how the word **love** is used in the first sentence of this Scripture. It's not future tense (you will love) or past tense (you loved). It's written in present tense (you love God). That's reflective of an **ongoing relationship** that's happening right now and will continue to happen in the future.

Even though we didn't walk in person with Christ during his time on earth, we can enjoy a relationship with him in the present tense—**right now**—and can continue to grow in that relationship every day.

Grab your Bible and check out John 20:19-29. What finally convinced Thomas to believe?

_____

_____

_____

_____

_____

Who does Christ tell Thomas he's going to bless in the future?

_____

_____

_____

_____

_____

Now read 1 Peter 1:8-9 again. What are we filled with?

_____ a. Contempt

_____ b. Hiccups

_____ c. Glorious joy

_____ d. Insecurity

How are you "living out" the joy Christ has placed within you?

_____

_____

_____

_____

_____

List some Christians you know who are living out the joy of the Lord.

_____

_____

_____

_____

_____

BITE #4

Concerning this salvation, the prophets, who spoke of the grace that was to come to you, searched intently and with the greatest care, trying to find out the time and circumstances to which the Spirit of Christ in them was pointing when he predicted the sufferings of the Messiah and the glories that would follow.

1 Peter 1:10-11

When Peter mentions "the grace that was to come to you," he's referring to Jesus Christ—the Messiah who would suffer for each one of us—and who makes our salvation possible by **grace** that he gives to all who believe, confess their sins, and accept him as their **Savior**.

When you think about the torture and death Christ suffered so you could be forgiven and experience eternal life, how do you feel?

_____ a. I don't think about it too much; usually just around Easter.

_____ b. I've heard the crucifixion story so much it doesn't really impact me anymore.

_____ c. I'm overcome with gratitude and awe at this indescribable gift.

_____ d. I don't understand it.

Take a moment to write a short prayer focusing on two things:

1. Thanking Jesus for what he did for you, and

2. Asking him to help you never take his death and suffering for granted.

_____

_____

_____

_____

_____

_____

_____

Let's take another look at the Scripture:

Concerning this salvation, the prophets, who spoke of the grace that was to come to you, searched intently and with the greatest care, trying to find out the time and circumstances to which the Spirit of Christ in them was pointing when he predicted the sufferings of the Messiah and the glories that would follow.

1 Peter 1:10-11

Peter is encouraging his readers to realize that **they** (the believers) were bringing glory to Jesus after his death. The prophets who had foretold his sufferings years earlier wanted to know what kind of **glories** would occur after such a tragic death. They not only wondered about this, but Peter tells us they actively *searched* to learn more and to discover the far-reaching implications of God's words through them.

Check out what Jesus says in Matthew 13:17:

> For truly I tell you, many prophets and righteous people longed to see what you see but did not see it, and to hear what you hear but did not hear it.

Imagine God telling you to write a book. God gives you the words to write, and you do so. God gives you accurate insight about what will happen 250 years from now. You're amazed! Yet, you also know that you won't get to see it, hear it, or experience it in any way. How would you feel? (Mark all that apply.)

_____ a. Frustrated.

_____ b. Excited to be part of such a big plan.

_____ c. Curious and yearning to actually see what you've written about.

_____ d. Bored.

The Christians to whom Peter wrote this letter had the **privilege of understanding** what the prophets had written—even better than the prophets themselves. You have this same privilege. You have the entire Bible— available in student editions and several translations—to help you understand all the predictions made about Christ and how they actually came to pass. You also have a church, a youth group, and Bible studies available to help you live out what you learn and to help you apply the truth of the Bible into your lifestyle.

Rate yourself on how much you're taking advantage of the spiritual smorgasbord around you (a *smorgasbord* is a buffet with lots of choices).

_____a. I go to church; that's about it.

_____ b. I go to church and youth group or Bible study.

_____ c. I go to church, youth group or Bible study, and Sunday school.

_____ d. I do all of the above, plus I'm involved in a ministry (helping in the nursery, singing on the praise team, greeting, calling students who are absent, serving on my youth council, being in a school-related Bible club, etc.).

If you're not taking full advantage of the spiritual smorgasbord available to you, why not? (And if you are taking advantage of all that's offered to you, what kind of difference is it making in your life?)

_____

_____

_____

_____

_____

It was revealed to them that they were not serving themselves but you, when they spoke of the things that have now been told you by those who have preached the gospel to you by the Holy Spirit sent from heaven. Even angels long to look into these things.

1 Peter 1:12

The prophets who wrote the parts of the Bible that predicted Christ's coming, his suffering, and his resurrection, were **divinely inspired** by the Holy Spirit to write the details God gave them. The Holy Spirit also told them, though, that what they were writing would _not_ be fulfilled during their lifetime. As the prophets wrote what God directed them to write, they were keenly aware that they were writing for **future generations**—the believers in Peter's day—as well as for you, your family, and your friends.

How incredibly special this should make us feel! Having the entire Bible at our fingertips and the ability to study and understand it should…

_____ a. move us toward a more intimate relationship with Christ.

_____ b. inspire us to wear T-shirts with Bible verses on them.

_____ c. be counted as simply having another good book.

_____ d. make everyone want to go deep-sea scuba diving.

It's a fact: If you read and study the Bible, you _will_ grow **closer** to God! Many people know this but still don't do anything about it. List some common **excuses** people give for not reading the Bible and not taking time to grow closer to God.

Let's take a few minutes to see how well you know the Bible by taking this fun quiz.

1. List the four Gospels.

1. _____

2. _____

3. _____

4. _____

2. In what city was Jesus born?

_____ a. Bethlehem

_____ b. Jerusalem

_____ c. Galilee

_____ d. Nazareth

3. Who once persecuted Christians, was temporarily blinded, became an outspoken Christian evangelist, and wrote much of the New Testament?

_____

4. What's the name of the first book of the Bible?

_____

5. What's the name of the last book of the Bible?

_____

6. Who came to Jesus at night and said he didn't understand how to be reborn?

_____ a. David

_____ b. Samuel

_____ c. Mark

_____ d. Nicodemus

7. How many books of the Bible did the apostle John write?

_____

8. How many books are in the Bible?

_____ a. 29

_____ b. 66

_____ c. 73

_____ d. 141

9. How old was Jesus when he began his public ministry?

_____

10. Who—from the Old Testament—was placed in a basket as a baby in the river?

_____

Answers:

1. Matthew, Mark, Luke, and John. 2. Bethlehem, 3. Paul, 4. Genesis, 5. Revelation, 6. Nicodemus, 7. 5 (The Gospel of John, 1 John, 2 John, 3 John, Revelation, 8. 66, 9. 30, 10. Moses

Scoring:

Count how many questions you got right.

_____ • **Bible illiterate.** (Scored three or less.) You know about as much as someone who doesn't even own a Bible. But the good news is that you can know more! Develop a good habit of reading your Bible every day—even if it's only one chapter a day. You'll be surprised at how much you'll learn.

_____ • **Bible reader.** (Scored four to eight.) You read the Bible some, but you're not really studying it, and you're probably not reading it consistently. Bible studies—such as the one you're doing right now—will give you a better understanding of what you're reading and will help you remember it better.

_____ • **Bible scholar.** (Scored nine or ten.) You enjoy reading your Bible and remember what you've studied. You're probably also involved in church and are growing in your relationship with Christ. Continue your pursuit of biblical knowledge. His Word is your flashlight and will help you see your pathway more clearly.

BITE #5

At the end of 1 Peter 1:12, the apostle tells us, "even angels long to look into these things."

This reminds us that angels are **not equal** to God. God knows all; angels do not. God is all-powerful; angels aren't. God has always been; God created angels; therefore they have *not* always been in existence.

The angels watch the **mystery of salvation** unfold in the lives of believers around the world. But as they watch, they are outsiders. Angels are often sent to minister to Christians as we struggle through trials and persecution, but they're **not** involved in **granting** salvation.

The angels also know that Christians are recipients of God's grace and some day will be highly honored in heaven. Because angels are spiritual beings, they don't need the blood of Christ to save them. And Peter is reminding the Christians that we have something even the angels don't have—salvation and grace. And then he tells us the angels long to understand this process. In other words, they have a strong desire to watch the plan of salvation unfold in the lives of Christians.

The angels were interested in Peter's readers. The angels are interested in **you** and your relationship with Christ. They're excited to watch you grow stronger in your faith. The Bible tells us that all of heaven breaks loose in a giant **party** when someone gives his or her life to the Lord. To put it another way, the angels go **wild**!

They're your cheerleaders. They get really, really, really jazzed when you make godly decisions and do what's right and depend on God!

This is going to **stretch** your mind a bit, but take a few minutes to create a cheer (and insert your name) of how an angel might respond to your spiritual growth.

_____

_____

_____

_____

Therefore, with minds that are alert and fully sober, set your hope on the grace to be brought to you when Jesus Christ is revealed at his coming.

1 Peter 1:13

Whenever you read "therefore" as you're studying the Bible, it's important to realize there's always a reason it's *there for*. In this case, Peter uses "therefore" to connect his reader's challenge in verse 13 with the previous verse. We previously learned that the prophets **anxiously** wanted to understand all that God inspired them to write, and even the angels desire to understand the process of salvation. *Therefore*, we should show the same kind of **excitement**. Peter tells us to have "minds that are alert." So get ready to dive into the deep end of the spiritual ocean!

Circle all the phrases descriptive of preparing for action.

making a "to do list"

sleeping

sitting by the beach

snoring

wearing work gloves

rolling up your sleeves

watching television

assessing the situation

lifting weights

reading the Bible

other: _____

Peter not only tells us to prepare for action, but he commands us to prepare our minds for action. This refers to...

_____ a. memorizing the Ten Commandments in a foreign language.

_____ b. spiritual headaches.

_____ c. mental and spiritual attitudes.

_____ d. dreaming about God while you sleep.

BITE #6

As obedient children, do not conform to the evil desires
you had when you lived in ignorance.

1 Peter 1:14

Obedience is connected to **knowledge** and **will**. A
four-year-old may attempt to cross the street during rush
hour traffic and assume that all cars will stop for him.
He doesn't yet have the **knowledge** and understanding
of red and green lights. A ten-year-old, however, knows
and **understands** why he can't cross the street in heavy
traffic. Therefore, the ten-year-old is more likely to obey
the traffic laws than a four-year-old.

**Take a moment to list some things you know and
understand about God now—things that you didn't
know and understand when you were six.**

1._____

_____

2._____

_____

3._____

_____

4. _____

_____

5. _____

_____

6. _____

_____

7. _____

_____

Obeying Christ isn't always easy. Oftentimes obedience will conflict with our own desires. List three areas in your life where you struggle with obedience to God.

1. _____

_____

2. _____

_____

3. _____

_____

Let's **eavesdrop** on a conversation between Christ and his heavenly Father in John 12:27-28:

"Now my soul is troubled, and what shall I say? 'Father, save me from this hour'? No, it was for this very reason I came to this hour. Father, glorify your name!"

What's Jesus talking about with his Father?

_____ a. Getting along with the disciples.

_____ b. Death by crucifixion.

_____ c. Wearing a different robe.

_____ d. What food would be served at the Last Supper.

Though human, Jesus didn't want to experience the pain of crucifixion, he wanted to obey his Father. You, too, will experience conflict between your own desires and obeying God. When you struggle with that, remember that the disciple who obeys God is one who:

_____ a. speaks a heavenly language;

_____ b. cares about what the angels think;

_____ c. truly loves God; or

_____ d. never misses church services.

Flip to John 14:21 for the answer.

As you're reading John 14:21 in your own Bible, what benefit does Jesus give of obeying him?

_____

_____

_____

_____

Now turn to Psalm 119:2. Who is called blessed?

_____

_____

_____

_____

Check out Psalm 119:20: "My soul is consumed with longing for your laws at all times." What would it take for you to _long_ for God's laws; to be consumed with obeying God?

_____

_____

_____

_____

_____

In the space below, write an email to God, asking him to help you desire obedience more than anything else in your life.

BITE #7

But just as he who called you is holy, so be holy in all you do; for it is written: "Be holy, because I am holy."

1 Peter 1:15-16

According to the above verse, we really don't have an excuse for these: (Circle all that apply.)

gossiping   stealing   hating a classmate

Bullying   being mean

dishonoring parents   cursing   lying

So if God commands us to be holy—just as God is holy— how come we still mess up? (Mark all that apply.)

_____ a. Because we're not perfect.

_____ b. Because we really don't care.

_____ c. Because we're still human.

_____ d. Because we've never really understood the command.

_____ e. Because holiness is something only angels can attain.

_____ f. Because we haven't fully surrendered to Christ's authority.

To understand what it means to be **holy,** we need to understand a little more about **God.**

Though God is one being, there are **three** distinct parts of God. This is called the **trinity**. The trinity consists of God, Jesus, and the Holy Spirit. They're not three separate gods—they're all part of the one true God—yet three distinct parts to whom Christians pray and worship. Sound confusing?

This is a hard concept to grasp for a lot of people! And you know what? We're not truly going to understand it until we get to heaven. So by faith simply accept the fact that God is ONE, yet there are three distinct parts that make up the one.

When you confessed your sins and asked Christ to reign in your life, he forgave your sins and lovingly invaded your heart with his presence. You didn't get just a little bit of God; you got **all of God**—all three parts of God!

As a new Christian, you probably started reading your Bible, praying, and going to church. As a result of having fellowship with Jesus, you began to **grow** in your relationship with him. As we grow closer to Jesus and get to know him better, he reveals different areas of our lives that aren't pleasing to him. As he does this, we have a choice:

1. We can either obey and confess that area of weakness to him and allow him to change us; or
2. We can disobey and serve Christ with only part of our lives, while refusing to allow him complete control.

If we choose the latter, Jesus isn't truly LORD of our life. We have all of him, but he doesn't have all of us!

There's no way you can be holy—as he is holy—in your own strength. To be truly holy would take some kind of **supernatural** power! Guess what—that's where the **Holy Spirit** comes in.

But to be filled and energized and saturated and guided with the power of the Holy Spirit requires **total surrender**. When you realize this, you don't have to start all over again, asking God to help you become a Christian. You're already a Christian. God has forgiven your sins; you simply aren't living in total surrender to God's Lordship.

Christ will always meet you **right where you are**. You can thank him again for forgiving your sins, and you can tell him you want him to be Lord of your life.

What does it mean to make Jesus Lord of your life?

_____

_____

_____

_____

Would you like to pray about making him Lord right now? If so, you can use this prayer:

Dear Jesus:

Thanks for forgiving my sins and coming into my life. I realize, though, that I haven't given you complete control of my whole life. I want to do that right now. I want you to be in charge. I relinquish control of my past, my present, and my future to you. Will you cleanse me and sanctify me within? I'd love for you to give me a spiritual bubble bath right now in the very depths of my being. Jesus, I give you my desires, my will, and my goals. I want to live for you with 100 percent commitment. Release the power of your Holy Spirit within me, and help me to rely on that power to resist temptation. In your holy name I pray, amen.

Take a second to jot down the implications of what you just did.

_____

_____

_____

_____

Check this out:

> I pray that you will begin to understand how incredibly great his power is to help those who believe him. It is that same mighty power that raised Christ from the dead.
>
> Ephesians 1:19-20, The Living Bible

WOW! The same mighty power that raised Christ from the dead and hung the stars in the sky and healed blind people is now in **you**! That's a lot of power! You don't want that power to just sit inside you and be dormant, do you?

No! You want to **use** that power and **live** in that power every single day of your life. How can do you that? By reading the Bible and praying every day—**that's** where your strength comes from. That's what keeps the Holy Spirit's power **activated** in you. In God's power you can say **no** to temptation. You no longer have to be a slave to sin!

Does this mean you'll never sin again? No, it means you don't have to **give in** to sin. But you're still human. You may still sin. If you do, you don't need to start all over and ask God to make you a Christian again. Remember, God will always meet you **right where you are**! So if you do sin, what should you do?

Let's look at 1 John 2:1 for the answer: "My dear children, I write this to you so that you will not sin."

The apostle John is telling us that we don't **have** to sin! By yielding to the power of the Holy Spirit within us, and by letting God be in complete control of our lives, we **can** say no to sin. But let's look at the rest of that verse. Check out what John goes on to say: "But if anybody does sin, we have an advocate with the Father—Jesus Christ, the Righteous One."

Whew! We're human. We'll still blow it. And when we do, there's always someone to whom we can turn— that someone is Jesus Christ, who's always willing to forgive a **repentant** heart.

What's the difference in **genuine repentance** and an attitude that says, "I'll ask God to forgive me today, but I'm going to go ahead and commit this particular sin tomorrow because God will just keep forgiving me?"

In which of the following two scenarios does Becca exhibit true repentance?

1. "Becca!" her sister Haley screamed. "I've told you a million times not to wear my pink sweater. And I can tell you've worn it because I see some of your hair on the back."

   "I'm sorry, Haley. It was two days ago. I was going to Marissa's birthday party and didn't have anything clean to wear. And the theme colors were pink and green. So I just grabbed your pink sweater to wear with my green khakis."

   "Okay. I forgive you. But Becca, please don't borrow it any more!"

That evening Becca got a call from her best friend, Emma. "Becca, you know that new cupcake store that just opened on Morgan Street?"

"Yeah! We've talked about getting some cupcakes there."

"Well, guess what? They're having a grand opening right now. Their décor colors are pink and brown. And anyone wearing pink who comes into the store right now will get a dozen free mini cupcakes. I'm wearing my pink shoes. Meet you there in five, okay?"

"You got it!" Becca said. "I know exactly what I'll wear." She headed to Haley's closet and grabbed the pink sweater. *Haley has such a soft heart, though. I'll just apologize again, and everything will be fine.*

* * *

2. "Becca!" her sister Haley screamed. "I've told you a million times not to wear my pink sweater. And I can tell you've worn it because I see some of your hair on the back."

"I'm sorry, Haley. It was two days ago. I was going to Marissa's birthday party and didn't have anything clean to wear. And the theme colors were pink and green. So I just grabbed your pink sweater to wear with my green khakis."

"Okay. I forgive you. But Becca, please don't borrow it any more!"

That evening Becca got a call from her best friend, Emma. "Becca, you know that new cupcake store that just opened on Morgan Street?"

"Yeah! We've talked about getting some cupcakes there."

"Well, guess what? They're having a grand opening right now. Their décor colors are pink and brown. And anyone wearing pink who comes into the store right now will get a dozen free mini cupcakes. I'm wearing my pink shoes. Meet you there in five, okay?"

"You go ahead, Emma. We only have one pink clothing item in our family, and it's my sister's sweater. I'm not supposed to borrow it."

"Ah, Haley's a big softie," Emma said. "She'll forgive you. Wear it now and apologize later."

"I wore it a couple of days ago to Marissa's party, and Haley already forgave me. When I apologized to her, I meant it."

"Yes, you meant it. But that doesn't mean you won't mean it again, too! Come on!"

"No, Emma. I really can't. I need to *show* Haley I mean I'm truly sorry by not doing it again. It's one thing to say I'm sorry and keep borrowing her sweater. It's another thing to say I'm sorry and show her I mean it by never borrowing her sweater again. You go on without me."

* * *

True repentance means that you don't plan on doing that particular thing again. You're truly sorry and you're proving it by your change of actions and behavior.

BITE #8

Since you call on a Father who judges each person's work impartially, live out your time as foreigners here in reverent fear.

1 Peter 1:17

What does it mean to "judge each person's work impartially?"

_____

_____

_____

God doesn't play **favorites**, nor does God judge on a point system. The person next to you won't receive more love from God because she's a **better student,** has more appealing features, or has a more outgoing personality. God loves each one of us **equally**, and God is a fair and just ruler, **full of patience**.

What does Peter mean when he encourages believers to live their lives as "foreigners here?"

_____

_____

_____

_____

Again, think of yourself as an "alien" living in only a temporary dwelling place—Earth. Maybe you've heard this slogan or have seen it on T-shirts: NOTW. It stands for "Not Of This World." Which person below is living with an "alien attitude"?

Fifteen-year-old Chloe and her family are missionaries living in Bolivia. There aren't any North Americans living in her small town. Chloe attends school and church with Bolivians. "I'm friends with many of the Bolivian girls," she says "but they'll never accept me as much as they do other Bolivians. And I'm okay with that. I'm never going to be a true Bolivian," she says with a laugh.

"Every three years our family takes a sabbatical and goes back home to Spokane, Washington. I enjoy the big youth group in our church there, but being away for three years at a time is hard. So even though I make a few friends, I never really fit in. I don't know the latest slang or trends or what's cool."

She laughs again. "I guess I'm always just an outsider," she says. "But you know what? I'm okay with it. I'm happy. I know God is with me."

* * *

Candice and her family just moved from Arizona to Florida, and she's not happy. "This is the worst thing that's ever happened to me," she says. "I don't have any friends. I've tried getting to know kids at school, but they all just see me as 'the new girl.' I've gone to a Bible study a few times at church, but kids there already know each other, and it's hard to break in.

"I hate my life!" Candice says. "I want badly to belong. I'll do anything!"

Two weeks later at school, she noticed a small group of girls lighting up in the bathroom. "Want a puff" they said when she walked in.

This is it, Candice thought. *This is my chance to fit in.* Even though Candice didn't want to smoke, she went ahead and joined simply because she was desperate to be included.

* * *

When you truly live as a "stranger" in this world, you're not desperate to fit it. You realize you don't actually belong here anyway; your real home is in heaven.

"Reverent fear" isn't being afraid of God as a slave would fear his master. "Reverent fear" is a healthy respect for your loving savior, acknowledging God's **authority** and power. God is our authority and our **judge**. Yes, we are privileged to be called God's **children**, but we can't assume this special title gives us permission to do whatever we want. That's not living in **reverent fear** of God.

What are three ways you can show reverent fear of God?

1. _____

_____

2. _____

_____

3. _____

_____

> For you know that it was not with perishable things such as silver or gold that you were redeemed from the empty way of life handed down to you from your ancestors; but with the precious blood of Christ, a lamb without blemish or defect. He was chosen before the creation of the world, but was revealed in these last times for your sake.
>
> 1 Peter 1:18-20

Perfect blood was needed to pay the penalty for your sins. Only Christ's blood is perfect—non-contaminated. And he willingly shed his own blood to pay the ransom price for your sin. He chose to suffer that we might be given total **freedom**.

Peter says, "He was chosen before the creation of the world." Before God even created darkness and light, God knew he would create **you**. God also knew you wouldn't be perfect—you'd be tainted with sin. So before God created animals, humans, mountains, or oceans, God knew he would give part of himself—God's only son—to stand in your place for the death penalty of sin.

In other words, God didn't decide to save you from your sins when he saw the world going **crazy**. He planned from the very beginning to be your sacrifice, because God's love for you is so great! You weren't an **afterthought** to God. Your salvation is so important to God that he created the **strategy**—or plan—for it before he even created the world!

If your non-Christian friends realized this, what kind of difference would it make in their lives?

_____

_____

_____

Through him you believe in God, who raised him from the dead and glorified him, and so your faith and hope are in God.

1 Peter 1:21

If you truly place your hope and faith in God, you're trusting in someone who is **all-powerful** and **all-knowing**. Think about it: If God can create the world, raise Christ from the dead, and cleanse you from sin, is there anything God *can't* do? What kind of perspective does this put on your times of **doubt**?

BITE #9

Now that you have purified yourselves by obeying the truth so that you have sincere love for each other, love one another deeply, from the heart.

1 Peter 1:22

What does it mean to love "from the heart?"

_____

_____

_____

Let's take a peek at 1 John 3:18:

Dear children, let us not love with words or speech but with actions and in truth.

Read these two scenarios and mark **"W"** or **"A"** to describe love in **words** or love in **action**.

Amber's family had just moved to New Jersey from California. She was nervous about attending a new school, finding a new church, and making new friends. The first Sunday they visited a church close to their new home, Amber met Monica and discovered they'd be attending the same high school.

This is great! Amber thought. *Monica's plugged into the youth group and may even be in some of my classes at school. It will be great to have someone to hang out with so quickly.*

When church was over, Monica turned to Amber and said, "It was great to meet you! You're gonna love our school. Maybe I'll see you in the cafeteria tomorrow."

Is Monica loving with words or with action?

      W   A

* * *

As Amber's family approached their car in the parking lot, Amber was caught off guard by someone rushing to her side. "Hey," a girl panted. "I raced out of the choir room as soon as I could. My name's Samantha, but you can call me Sam."

"Hi, Sam!" Amber had to laugh as the girl tried to catch her breath. "You must be on the track team."

"No way," Sam giggled. "If I were an athlete, I wouldn't be so out of breath. I'm on the praise team, and we were rehearsing a few new songs. I just wanted to catch you before you left. I heard you'll be attending Central High School. I go there, too!"

"Really?" Amber was all ears. "Is it a good school?"

"Oh, yeah! You're gonna love it," Sam said. "But I only moved here a couple of years ago, and I remember how weird it was not knowing anyone. So if you want, I'll be glad to pick you up tomorrow morning. But don't expect anything great," Sam laughed and grinned. "My car's a hand-me-down from my great-aunt Clara. Anyway, I'll be glad to help you find your classes."

"Really?" Amber was excited.

"Sure! And let's just plan on meeting in the cafeteria under the big clock at noon so you won't have to eat alone. I'll introduce you to everyone."

Amber was so relieved. "Thanks, Jesus," she silently prayed as she climbed into her parents' car to head home.

Is Samantha loving with words or with action?

W   A

Describe how someone specifically loved you with action.

_____

_____

_____

_____

_____

Now take a moment to describe how you loved someone in word only, when you could have gone a step further and loved him or her with your actions.

_____

_____

_____

_____

_____

Describe the difference it makes when you express love with words or express love in action.

_____

_____

_____

_____

_____

For you have been born again, not of perishable seed, but of imperishable, through the living and enduring word of God.

1 Peter 1:23

When you became a Christian, you started a new life. This new life was given to you by…

_____ a. your parents.

_____ b. your grandparents.

_____ c. your pastor.

_____ d. your Heavenly Father.

The life your parents gave you will someday end, but the life you have in Jesus Christ will last **forever**.

> For, "All people are like grass, and all their glory is like the flowers of the field; the grass withers and the flowers fall, but the word of the Lord endures forever." And this is the word that was preached to you.
>
> 1 Peter 1:24-25

Because everything in our earthly life is only **temporary,** it makes sense to stop spending so much energy and time on things of the world and focus more **intently** on Jesus and his **eternal kingdom**.

What are two "temporary" things you could spend less time on so you could focus more on Christ?

1._____

2._____

What will it take for you to make this change?

_____

_____

_____

_____

_____

Will you do it?

_____

_____

_____

_____

_____

BITE #10

Grab a Friend

You did it! You made it all the way through the first chapter of 1 Peter. You're a Secret Power Girl who is growing closer to Christ because you're taking his Word seriously. Now grab a friend and discuss the following questions together.

Peter reminds us that we are merely "foreigners in the world." We therefore need to focus less attention on temporary things and zero in on that which is eternal. What things should I have spent less time on this week? Am I truly learning to focus more on eternal things?

@ Was there a time this week I deliberately chose to focus on that which is eternal?

@ How have I displayed self-control this week?

@ In what ways am I taking advantage of the "spiritual smorgasbord" around me? How can I more fully use this smorgasbord?

@ How specifically did I love "from the heart" this week?

@ In what ways did I love with action? Were there times I also loved in word only?

@ How can I consciously move to more heart-loving and less word-loving?

Memorize It!

Try to memorize this passage with your friend and say it to each other the next time you get together:

> But just as he who called you is holy, so be holy in all you do; for it is written: "Be holy, because I am holy."
>
> 1 Peter 1:15-16

My Journal

Okay, S.P.G., this is your space, so take advantage of it. You can do whatever you want here, but always try to include the following:

@ List your prayer requests. (Later, as God answers them, go back and record the date when God answered your prayer.)

© Copy down any verse we studied in the previous chapter that you don't understand. Then let this be a reminder to ask your parents, Sunday school teacher, pastor, or youth leader about it.

© Jot down what stood out the most from this section.

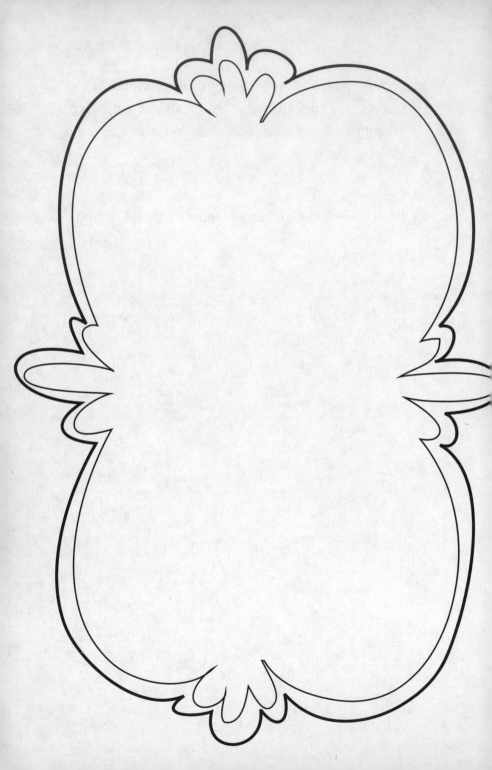

Sometimes It's Okay to Be a Crybaby

1 Peter 2:1-25

BITE #1

Therefore, rid yourselves of all malice and all deceit, hypocrisy, envy, and slander of every kind.

1 Peter 2:1

What are other ways to describe "rid yourselves of?" (Circle all that apply.)

run a marathon

put away

purify

go shopping

walk the dog

clean your room

remove

put off

bake cookies

practice the piano

erase from your life

take off

let go of

throw away

Peter tells us to rid ourselves of malice, deceit, hypocrisy, envy, and slander. Let's make sure we know what we're talking about before we go any further. See if you can match the correct definition with the words listed.

_____ 1. Malice

a. To destroy someone's good reputation by spreading rumors or lies.

_____ 2. Deceit

b. Saying one thing but doing the opposite.

_____ 3. Hypocrisy

c. Desiring something that someone else has to the point of causing resentment.

_____ 4. Envy   d. The desire to harm others; doing evil to someone.

_____ 5. Slander   e. Deliberately misleading someone by lying or skirting the truth.

(You can find the correct answers at the end of Bite #1.)

Take a peek at 1 Peter 2:1 again. If you're having trouble ridding yourself of "all malice, all deceit, hypocrisy, envy, and slander of every kind," first commit those areas to Christ and ask for his forgiveness. Then consider doing what a few other teen girls have done. Read the examples below and mark one that you'd like to try.

The problem: COVET.
Abby couldn't stand the way Alicia always flaunted her new things. It didn't matter what it was—new sweater, new shoes, new iPad—she always bragged about them to Abby, whose parents could barely afford to purchase her a pair of sneakers for gym class. "There were times," Abby said, "that I wanted to rip her sweater or smash her iPad, but not anymore."

The solution: "First I asked God to forgive me," Abby says, "because I knew what I was feeling wasn't right. And then I asked my mom to hold me accountable. We prayed together every morning before school, and after school she'd ask me how I treated Abby and what I felt. Knowing Mom was going to be asking me the tough questions, helped me keep my feelings in check. Now Mom and I talk about other stuff, but it no longer bugs me that Abby has stuff I'll never have."

The problem: DECEIT.

"Do you have your homework finished, Shayna?" Mom called from the bottom of the stairs.

"Are you kidding?" Shayna replied. "I know the consequences of not finishing my homework on time."

Shayna turned out the lights and went to bed with a pile of homework still unfinished. She felt guilty about deceiving her mom, but it wasn't like she actually said, "Yes, I've finished my homework."

The next morning her mom handed her a bagel at the kitchen table and said, "Shayna, you haven't finished your homework, have you?"

Shayna almost choked on her bagel. How did her mom know? "Uh . . . well, not exactly."

"Shayna, you lied to me."

"No, I didn't, Mom."

"Yes, you really did, honey. When you deceive someone, it's the same as lying. Get your homework out, and I'll help you finish it before you leave for school, but I want you to realize how serious lying is."

"It's not that big of a deal."

"Yes, it is," Mom said. "I've noticed you've been

lying a lot lately, even over small stuff."

"Wow. I didn't realize that," Shayna said. "It's not that I want to lie, Mom. I just . . . I don't know."

"It's an easy trap to fall into. But if you don't overcome it now, it'll only get worse as you get older. If you really want to stop, I think I can help."

The solution: "Okay. What do I do?"

"Well, first of all, we're going to ask God to forgive you for lying. Then we're going to ask him to help you stop." At that point, Shayna's mom pulled a rubber band out of the kitchen drawer and put it on her daughter's wrist. "This," her mom explained, "is your reminder not to lie."

"A rubber band?"

"That's right. Shayna, every single time you're tempted to deceive someone, pop this rubber band against your wrist."

"Ow! That's gonna hurt!"

"Exactly."

"Oh, I get it. And eventually, I'll break the habit of lying."

"That's right!"

The problem: ENVY.

"How many friends are you having at your birthday party, Julie?" Mandie asked her little sister.

"I haven't sent out the invitations yet, but I think

I'm inviting seven." The two girls talked about who would be coming, the games they'd play, movies they'd watch, and kind of pizza they'd order.

"Hey, Julie, I just realized you didn't put Erin's name on your list."

"Yeah, I'm not inviting her."

"Why not, sis? I thought you two were friends."

"Well, we are. But she has all the latest Wii games, and a cool flat screen in her bedroom, and she even has more than 80 apps on her phone!"

"Wow. That's amazing. But what does that have to do with not inviting her to your party?"

"Whenever I'm around her, I get mad at her because she has all this cool stuff that I'd like to have."

"Sounds like you're envious, sis."

"Maybe I am. But it bothers me so much that I don't even want to be with her anymore."

"I used to be envious of Hannah."

"You're kidding! She's your best friend."

"She is now, but she wouldn't be if I hadn't taken care of my envy. I was jealous of her musical ability forever."

"How'd you get over being envious?" Julie asked?

The solution: "I prayed for her."

"Why?"

"Because it's impossible to be envious of someone you're praying for. It didn't happen overnight. In fact, it took a few months. But I'm no longer envious of her. If you want to stop being envious, Julie, first ask God to forgive you. Then ask him to help you. And the more you pray for Erin, the less envy you'll have."

These three solutions will work for any of the things Peter is telling us to rid ourselves of. Will you try them?

Christians should have no part in malice, envy, hypocrisy, deceit, or slander. Our goal is to reflect our Heavenly Father. Check out Ephesians 5:1. According to this verse, who are you to imitate?

_____

_____

_____

To live with malice, deceit, hypocrisy, envy, or slander is to live like the world. God has a higher calling on your life! God calls you to holiness (1 Peter 1:16). Grab your Bible and flip to Romans 12:1-2. According to this verse, how much like the world does God want you to be?

_____

_____

_____

_____

According to Romans 12:2, what does God call you to do?

_____

_____

_____

_____

_____

Read Romans 12:2 one more time. How can we know God's will?

_____

_____

_____

_____

> Like newborn babies, crave pure spiritual milk, so that by it you may grow up in your salvation, now that you have tasted that the Lord is good.
>
> 1 Peter 2:2-3

Circle some of your favorite drinks.

herbal tea Gatorade Cherry Coke

Vanilla Coke Hot chocolate Grape juice

Orange juice Hot water Raspberry lemonade Warm milk

Frappuccino Grapefruit juice Ginger Ale

Iced tea Coffee Cold water Apple juice

Eggnog Root Beer Dr. Pepper

Hot tea Cold milk

Sprite 7-Up Tomato juice Orange soda

Coca-Cola

Just as **milk** is full of nutrients and makes a growing baby healthy, Christ has given you nutrients through a relationship with him and his Word. Have you ever been so **thirsty** that your mouth was dry and felt like it was stuffed full of cotton? A glass of cold water can quickly **quench** your thirst.

What's the longest you've gone without water?

_____

_____

What's the longest you've gone without any kind of liquid drink?

_____

_____

Jesus wants you to thirst for **him**. He wants you to be so thirsty for him that your soul truly longs to be **quenched** by his Word. Is this how you view the Bible? Do you see God's Word—and your relationship with Christ—as the only thing that will truly satisfy your thirst? If not, take a few moments to write a prayer in the space provided and ask Jesus to help you develop a thirst for him. If you're already **thirsty** for him, write a prayer asking him to help you to find satisfaction from his Word for your thirst.

(Answers to the quiz on p. 80: 1. d   2. e   3. b   4. c   5. a)

BITE #2

As you come to him, the living Stone—rejected by humans but chosen by God and precious to him—you also, like living stones, are being built into a spiritual house to be a holy priesthood, offering spiritual sacrifices acceptable to God through Jesus Christ.

1 Peter 2:4-5

Notice how Peter begins this verse: "As you come to him." You've already come to Jesus for your salvation, but this Scripture assures us that we are to continue coming to him for all our needs. As you continue coming to Christ on a daily basis, you can't help but grow spiritually. To continually come to Christ is to be in his presence; to draw near to him; to enjoy fellowship with him. In fact, you come to Christ so often during the day that it becomes as natural as breathing. List some things you do so often every day that you hardly think about them anymore; they've just become a natural part of your daily routine.

1. _____

2. _____

3. _____

4. _____

5. _____

Next, Peter describes Christ as being a "living Stone." Peter wasn't making this up. He'd heard Jesus use this very description of himself during his time on earth. Let's check out Matthew 21:42:

> Jesus said to them, "Have you never read in the Scriptures: 'The stone the builders rejected has become the cornerstone; the Lord has done this, and it is marvelous in our eyes'?"

Who was the "stone the builders rejected"?

_____ a. Your fifth-grade teacher

_____ b. Jesus

_____ c. Your next-door neighbor

_____ d. Justin Timberlake

Jesus was referring to what had been foretold of him. Let's take a peek at Psalm 118:22-23 for the proof:

> The stone the builders rejected has become the cornerstone; the Lord has done this, and it is marvelous in our eyes.

Don't you love it when we tie the Old Testament and the New Testament together? **God's Word is absolute truth!** Though it was written over a span of several centuries, every word was God-inspired.

Many Christians mistakenly believe the Old Testament isn't as important as the New Testament, because it was written before Jesus walked on earth. But both the Old and New Testaments are necessary ingredients for every Christian's spiritual growth. Mark all the statements that are descriptive of you.

_____ a. I've read the entire Old Testament.

_____ b. I've read the entire New Testament.

_____ c. I understand the New Testament better than I understand the Old Testament.

_____ d. I love the stories in the Old Testament.

_____ e. I don't get the Old Testament at all.

_____ f. I find portions of the Old Testament boring, but I know it's important that I read it.

If you've never read the **entire Bible**, challenge yourself to do that this year! Here's how: If you'll read just three chapters every single day (Monday through Saturday) and five chapters every Sunday, you'll automatically have the entire Bible read in exactly one year!

Several times during his ministry on earth, Jesus tied the Old Testament into his teaching. If Jesus needed and valued the **Old Testament**, so should we! In fact, we need the whole Bible. Reading God's Holy Word is **essential** to your spiritual growth!

Read 2 Timothy 3:16-17:

All Scripture is God-breathed and is useful for teaching, rebuking, correcting and training in righteousness, so that the servant of God may be thoroughly equipped for every good work.

According to the above verse, do we have any excuse for *not* reading and studying the entire Bible?

Let's take another look at the same verse in a different version of the Bible:

The whole Bible was given to us by inspiration from God and is useful to teach us what is true and to make us realize what is wrong in our lives; it straightens us out and helps us do what is right. It is God's way of making us well prepared at every point, fully equipped to do good to everyone."

2 Timothy 3:16-17, The Living Bible

Based on the above Scripture, list six things you'll gain when you read and study the Bible.

1. _____

2. _____

3. _____

4. _____

5. _____

6. _____

Let's take another peek at what Peter wrote:

As you come to him, the living Stone—rejected by humans but chosen by God and precious to him—you also, like living stones, are being built into a spiritual house to be a holy priesthood, offering spiritual sacrifices acceptable to God through Jesus Christ.

1 Peter 2:4-5

We are called "living stones." In other words, God wants to take your "living stone" (your life) and **build you** into a strong spiritual house. We know that cement, mortar, concrete, and other supplies make strong bricks. What are some **elements** you'll need to use to make yourself a strong spiritual stone?

_____

_____

_____

_____

_____

Ask yourself this question: "Am I willing to be shaped and molded into the kind of spiritual stone God wants me to be?" Notice, God isn't calling you to be the whole **temple** or the cornerstone; that's Christ's position. Jesus simply wants all of you to be like **modeling clay** in his holy hands, willing to be broken, molded, and reshaped for his **purposes** and glory.

Peter also tells the believers that we are to be "a holy priesthood." This is an offering, a spiritual sacrifice. By allowing God to do whatever God wants to with our lives, we are offering ourselves to God as **living sacrifices**.

Let's take another look at how different portions of the Bible complement each other. Check out Romans 12:1:

> Therefore, I urge you, brothers and sisters, in view of God's mercy, to offer your bodies as a living sacrifice, holy and pleasing to God—this is your true and proper worship.

Quick recap: What's the living sacrifice?

_____ a. My life.

_____ b. My school.

_____ c. My iPod.

_____ d. My best friend.

It's not simply yourself that's the living sacrifice: it's all you do. Grab your Bible and flip to Hebrews 13:15-17. What activities do these verses mention that we can give as a pleasing sacrifice?

_____

_____

_____

_____

_____

According to Scripture, **every area** of our lives—our sports, our friendships, our attitudes, our clothing—can and **should** be given as a living sacrifice to God. Think about your day. In all you've done and all you've thought about, identify some living sacrifices you manifested in the past 12 hours that were pleasing to God.

BITE #3

For in Scripture it says: "See, I lay a stone in Zion, a chosen and precious cornerstone, and the one who trusts in him will never be put to shame." Now to you who believe, this stone is precious. But to those who do not believe, "The stone the builders rejected has become the cornerstone," and, "a stone that causes people to stumble and a rock that makes them fall." They stumble because they disobey the message—which is also what they were destined for.

1 Peter 2:6-8

Peter is quoting from Isaiah 28:16. When talking to others about Christ, strive to support your witness by the Word of God. If the philosophy or teaching you're presenting can't be backed up with Scripture, **think twice** before saying it!

Grab your Bible and find 1 John 4:1-3. What advice does John give for knowing what to believe?

_____

_____

_____

_____

_____

Have you ever believed something that was false? Describe the situation.

_____

_____

_____

_____

Peter's witness was **stronger** with the people to whom he was writing, because he backed up what he said with other portions of **Scripture**. Jesus is referred to as the cornerstone, which is the first stone laid in a building. This stone is the **beginning** of the new work. It's the **start** of the project that will someday be completed.

Christ is the cornerstone in your spiritual life. He is the beginning of all God wants to complete in your life. As you continue your relationship with Christ, **God is faithful** to consistently build upon you as a living stone, useful for God's Kingdom.

What promise does Peter say we have if we believe in Jesus as our cornerstone and place our faith in him alone?

_____

_____

_____

This doesn't mean that Christians will never have problems. The name of this chapter is "Sometimes It's Okay to Be a Crybaby." The Christians to whom Peter wrote knew all about pain and suffering. They not only had been made fun of for their faith, but they also had been harshly criticized. No doubt they shed many tears through the hurt. It's okay to cry. God knows your hurt. Jesus certainly understands your pain. Check out Psalm 34:18: "The Lord is close to those whose hearts are breaking" (The Living Bible). How does that make you feel?

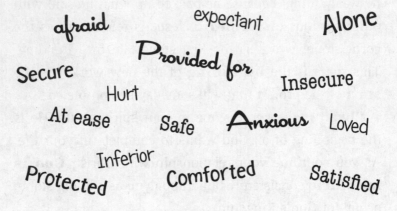

Briefly describe a time you felt your heart was breaking.

_____

_____

_____

_____

How did God help you through the above experience?

_____

_____

_____

_____

_____

We **will** have trials, face persecution, and feel disappointment. But our **trust in God** is never wrong; it's never misplaced. God will never, ever, **ever** let us down! Jesus is true to his Word, and he never breaks his promises. You can **depend** on him. You can **count** on him. He is absolutely **trustworthy**!

Identify a time in your life when you depended on God and learned from the experience.

_____

_____

_____

_____

_____

Peter goes on to remind the believers that we receive **honor** from God. But those who choose not to place their faith in Christ face a different result. They don't see Jesus as a precious stone. They choose, instead, to reject him— to toss him aside.

Christ referred to the "builders" who rejected him as the religious leaders (Matthew 21:42). They **refused** to accept Jesus as the Son of God—as the cornerstone. Instead, they chose other things on which to build the foundation of their lives.

What are some typical other "foundations" your non-Christian friends choose to build their lives upon?

_____

_____

_____

_____

Peter then tells us that God has already planned **punishment** for those who disbelieve. But if we skip ahead to Peter's next letter, we're reminded how **patient** God is. Jesus truly wants **everyone** to believe in him and follow him, but he doesn't force anyone's decision. **Each person** must decide for herself whether she will accept Christ as Lord. Let's skip ahead to 2 Peter 3:9: "He is patient with you, not wanting anyone to perish, but everyone to come to repentance."

According to the above Scripture, what does God desire for everyone in the world?

_____

_____

_____

_____

_____

_____

BITE #4

> But you are a chosen people, a royal priesthood, a holy nation, God's special possession, that you may declare the praises of him who called you out of darkness into his wonderful light.
>
> 1 Peter 2:9

How does it make you feel to know that you've been chosen?

Treasured   Set apart   Valuable

Honored   Delighted   Special

Confused   Excited   Argumentative

Haphazard   Privileged

Worth a lot   Rejected   Nonchalant

Happy   Hateful   Grateful

Peter tells us to "declare the praises of him who called you out of darkness into his wonderful light." How do Christians declare God's praises?

_____

_____

_____

What does "called you out of darkness into his wonderful light" mean?

_____

_____

_____

What is a personal testimony?

_____ a. It's something that's used in court...I think.

_____ b. It's a secret.

_____ c. It's my story of how I came to know Jesus as Lord and Savior.

_____ d. It's the book I haven't written yet.

Have you ever written out your personal testimony?

Yes   No

Have you ever verbally shared your personal testimony?

Yes   No

Your personal testimony is comprised of **three parts,** and Peter has mentioned a **super important** portion of your testimony. Let's take an inside look at your testimony right now:

MY PERSONAL TESTIMONY

Part 1: My Life before Christ

(Go ahead. Jot down what you were like before Christ saved you from sin. Perhaps you were extremely self-centered, bullied people, disrespected others, etc.)

_____

_____

_____

_____

Part 2: How I Met Christ

(Now jot down the environment in which you asked Christ to come into your life and forgive your sins. Maybe you were at church camp, at a Christian concert, in your bedroom, etc.)

_____

_____

_____

_____

_____

Part 3: My Life after Christ

(Now describe the difference Christ is making in your life. Perhaps you sense a new meaning and purpose now; maybe he's changed your attitudes or helped you quit a specific habit, etc.)

_____

_____

_____

_____

_____

Guess what—that's your **testimony**! Strive to keep your testimony to three minutes or less, and ask God to give you opportunities to share it with your non-Christian friends.

BITE #5

Once you were not a people, but now you are the people of God; once you had not received mercy, but now you have received mercy.

1 Peter 2:10

Peter is helping the believers remember what God has done for them. It's important to remember where we came from so we will appreciate where we are now. In other words, count your blessings! What has God done for you recently? Have you taken the privilege of worship for granted? There are thousands of Christians who are being persecuted right now for their faith. Take a few minutes to count some of your blessings.

1. _____

_____

2. _____

_____

3. _____

_____

4. _____

_____

5._____

_____

6._____

_____

7._____

_____

8._____

_____

9._____

_____

10._____

_____

Dear friends, I urge you, as foreigners and exiles, to abstain from sinful desires, which wage war against your soul.

1 Peter 2:11

Thus far in Peter's letter, he has stressed holy living. Now he gets down to the basics: he gives us some practical tips on how to live holy lives. First, he reminds us that the earth isn't our real home. Though we live

on the earth 24/7 right now, it's simply a temporary dwelling place. Where is your real home—the place you'll live forever?

_____

_____

_____

Can you list three things that are eternal?

    1. _____

    2. _____

    3. _____

Can you list three things that are not eternal?

    1. _____

    2. _____

    3. _____

Since your real home is **heaven**, ask God to help you focus intently on what's **eternal** instead of getting caught up in the things of this world. What are some things that easily distract you from focusing on eternity?

Let's take another look at 1 Peter 2:11.

Dear friends, I urge you, as foreigners and exiles, to abstain from sinful desires, which wage war against your soul.

What does it mean to abstain?

_____ a. To blend in with.

_____ b. To bake at 350 degrees for 20 minutes.

_____ c. To stay away from.

_____ d. To wrap up and give away.

Why is it important to abstain from sinful desires? (Reread the verse again for the answer.)

_____

_____

_____

_____

As a follower of Christ, you'll constantly face temptation. So many distractions in life can get your attention away from Jesus. Worldly voices will tempt you, trip you, persecute you, and **lie to you** in order to weaken or dissolve your relationship with Jesus.

You were born with sinful desires, and though you currently live in a sinful world, you **can** surrender your worldly desires to the supernatural power of the Holy Spirit. You can't fight this battle in your own strength, and God doesn't expect you to! But through God's power, you truly can choose to abstain from evil.

For example, why choose to hang out with people who you know will start gossiping about others behind their backs? Though you can't help but live in a sinful world, you can choose **not** to place yourself right in the middle of sin.

Peter tells us to **abstain**. And it's not a one-time decision; abstaining must be a continuous decision! It requires **total submission** to the authority of God, not in just part of your life. This is **radical obedience**!

What are some specific things, temptations, or places that you may need to abstain from in order to be the holy disciple God is calling you to be?

_____

_____

_____

_____

Think back to your testimony—specifically to your life before you allowed Christ to take control. You should be able to see a defining **difference** in your life. In other words, there are some things you may have participated in as a non-Christian that Jesus is leading you **not** to participate in now. When Jesus becomes LORD of your life, he wants to produce **change**. If you continue in the same old lifestyle, same old habits, same old sin, it's obvious that you haven't allowed Jesus to **change** you. Therefore, you're not experiencing **new life** in Christ.

Let's take a moment right now to talk this over with him:

Dear Jesus:

I want to be all you call me to be. I want to live a holy life. And I'm making a conscious decision right now to abstain from the things you don't want me to participate in. If there's an area in my life to which I'm blinded, please bring it to my mind right now, and I'll commit that area to you. I want to be cleansed and changed from the inside out, and I want those around me to notice the difference you're continually making in my life. Thank you, Jesus! Amen.

BITE #6

Live such good lives among the pagans that, though they accuse you of doing wrong, they may see your good deeds and glorify God on the day he visits us.

1 Peter 2:12

Living a **good** life involves obedience to Christ and doing good things. Though it's not good things that save us (it's Christ's grace), he wants us involved in good work so that others may be ministered to by our **actions**.

What are some good things others have done that have ministered to you?

1._____

_____

_____

2._____

_____

_____

3._____

_____

_____

What good things have you done this week that have ministered to others?

1._____

_____

2._____

_____

3._____

_____

Our main goal as Christians is to glorify Christ in all we do. Hopefully, by living in such a way that brings honor to his name, others will be led into a relationship with him. Identify the words that describe how a Christian should live:

Harshly   Lovingly   Jealously

With integrity   Tenderly

Boastingly   Causing discord   Peacefully

Kindly   Honestly   Putting others first

> Submit yourselves for the Lord's sake to every human authority: whether to the emporer, as the supreme authority, or to governors, who are sent by him to punish those who do wrong and to commend those who do right.
>
> 1 Peter 2:13-14

Notice that God **doesn't** shine favor on one of type of government over another; God simply commands us to **accept the authority** of the government under which we live—though this doesn't mean we should obey the government if it requires we do something **immoral**.

Peter isn't encouraging a Christian to go against her **conscience**. Check out what Peter said when *he* faced criticism from the government: "We must obey God rather than human beings!" (Acts 5:29)

Two-thirds of the world's Christians today live under **repressive** government authority, and thousands are persecuted and even killed for their faith in Christ. Only one-third of today's Christians live in an area where they're free to worship Jesus and **openly** express their devotion to him.

Christ **doesn't** want you to obey a government that tries to force you to forsake your faith in him. But he **does** expect you to follow governmental standards that are best for the community (traffic laws, tax laws, etc.).

> For it is God's will that by doing good you should silence the ignorant talk of foolish people.
>
> 1 Peter 2:15

There's a common phrase used by Christian leaders in describing how we should live so that others may see our faith: *You may be the only Bible some people will ever see.* What do you think this means?

_____

_____

_____

_____

_____

Your lifestyle and actions are **louder** than your actual words. Peter has referred to Christians as "living stones." You can also be seen as a "living Bible" or a "living witness" for Christ. You may have some non-Christian friends who'd never consider going to church, but they're **watching your lifestyle** and eventually will become curious about your faith if you continue to live it out in front of them.

By living a **holy lifestyle** and making good deeds a part of your daily actions, no one will have reason to criticize you. If people *do* persecute you, it's better to be criticized for doing **good** than for breaking the law.

> Live as free people, but do not use your freedom as a cover-up for evil; live as God's slaves.
>
> 1 Peter 2:16

Yes, God has **freed** us from the bondage of sin. But that doesn't give us license to do whatever we want, thinking, *Hey! I've been set free! I can do whatever I want.* Peter continues to stress **holy living**, and all Christians are expected to live with the Ten Commandments as a **non-negotiable** moral code. Notice the Ten Commandments are not called Ten Suggestions; they're **commandments**, and every Christian should take them seriously.

Regarding the Ten Commandments...

_____ a. I know what they are and what they mean.

_____ b. I think I could list a few of them if I had to.

_____ c. I've never given them much thought.

_____ d. It would do me well to read them and take them more seriously.

For a quick refresher on the Ten Commandments, flip back to the Old Testament—Exodus 20:1-17.

BITE #7

Show proper respect to everyone, love the family of believers, fear God, honor the emporer.

1 Peter 2:17

To show respect means to...

_____ a. hold hands with, smile at, and sing to.

_____ b. value, esteem, and honor.

_____ c. tickle, scratch, and pinch.

_____ d. ridicule, harass, and berate.

How do you show respect to your teachers?

_____

_____

_____

How do you show respect to your parents?

_____

_____

_____

How do you show respect to your friends?

_____

_____

_____

How do you feel when someone acts disrespectfully toward you?

_____

_____

_____

Why is it so important to respect others?

_____

_____

_____

Peter tells us not only to respect people, but also to "love the family of believers." How does this tie in with living a holy life?

_____

_____

_____

We're told the world will know we're Christians by our...

_____ a. grades.

_____ b. fashion sense.

_____ c. jokes.

_____ d. love.

Even though the **body of Christ** is comprised of many different denominations, we are to love each other in spite of our disagreements and varying interpretations of Scripture. Most Christians and denominations actually have more in **common** than they have differences. Peter is encouraging us to focus on our common love and **devotion** to Christ rather than smaller details such as how a particular church body is governed, how many times communion is served, or the size of the buildings.

Next, Peter encourages us to "fear God." A **healthy** fear toward something leads to **obedience**. For example, if you see a sign that says, "Stay away; snakes are in this field!" you'd probably **obey** the sign because you have a **proper fear** of snakes.

Maintaining a proper fear of God helps us remember who we are and who God is. **God is God**; we are not. Jesus is the King of Kings and Lord of Lords. We're imperfect and weak humans.

How did Moses display proper fear when God appeared to him as a burning bush? (See Exodus 3:1-6.)

_____

_____

_____

Peter **repeats** the importance of respecting the government by telling us to "honor the emporer." Again, he's not encouraging Christians to go against their consciences or to obey a government that tells them to do something immoral, but we **are** to obey the laws of the land.

Grab your Bible and turn to Matthew 22:15-21. What did Jesus have to say about obeying the government in regard to taxes?

_____

_____

_____

Now flip to Romans 13:7. What does the apostle Paul say regarding the government and taxes?

_____

_____

_____

Perhaps you've heard of people who try to cheat the government by not reporting all they earn in an attempt to avoid paying as much tax as they're supposed to. Why is this wrong?

_____

_____

_____

_____

_____

BITE #8

Slaves, in reverent fear of God submit yourselves to your masters, not only to those who are good and considerate, but also to those who are harsh.

1 Peter 2:18

It's hard for us to relate to being a slave or having a slave. But we **can** identify with employers. While it's easy to respect a fair and kind employer, it's a lot tougher when the **employer** is harsh or plays favorites.

But again, you may be the only "Bible" your future employer will ever see. By being submissive to his authority and acting with integrity, you may eventually whet his appetite to know more about your relationship with Christ.

Mark all statements characteristic of an employee who acts with integrity and dependability.

_____ a. Showing up on time.

_____ b. Laughing at the gossip shared in the lounge.

_____ c. Responding with a good attitude when the boss gives you extra work.

_____ d. Leaving work a little early but not reporting it on your time sheet.

For it is commendable if someone bears up under the pain of unjust suffering because they are conscious of God.

1 Peter 2:19

This verse is a **continuation** of the previous admonishment to be submissive to our masters. Many of the early Christians were **household servants** or slaves. It was easy for them to get along with masters who were kind and considerate. But it was extremely difficult to endure **suffering** from an unjust master.

Slaves were considered property. Often a cruel master would beat or imprison a slave for no good reason. God never promised Christians that we'd have an easy life, but God **did** promise to be with us in the midst of our suffering and to provide strength and comfort.

Peter learned about suffering from Jesus himself, and he knew his Lord's suffering was part of God's plan. Grab your Bible and turn to Matthew 16:21-28. How did Jesus respond to Peter's suggestion of not letting him suffer?

_____

_____

_____

_____

_____

Jesus told his disciples to take up their crosses and follow him. He tells us the same thing today. Circle all phrases that help define what taking up the cross to follow him means.

Carrying a cross in your backpack

Buying a gold ring with a cross on it

Fierce loyalty

Realizing there is a risk in following Christ

True commitment

Dedication

Facing possible persecution for your faith

Singing songs with the word "cross" in them

No turning back

Wearing a silver cross around your neck

Tattooing a cross on your forehead

But how is it to your credit if you receive a beating for doing wrong and endure it? But if you suffer for doing good and you endure it, this is commendable before God.

1 Peter 2:20

It's not appropriate for Christians to expect praise for being punished for doing something wrong. That should be expected. If we're punished for doing what's right, however, we're **sharing** in the suffering of Christ.

Take a second to remember a time when you received deserved punishment for doing something wrong. What did you do?

_____

_____

_____

_____

What was your punishment?

_____

_____

_____

_____

Can you identify a time when you were punished for doing something _right_? If so, describe the situation and how it made you feel. If not, can you imagine a time when this might realistically happen?

_____

_____

_____

_____

When we make Jesus LORD of our lives, we surrender everything—including our rights. This is hard for many Christians to swallow, because we're bombarded with advertisements by people encouraging us to "demand our rights," "stand up for our rights," "claim what's rightfully ours." What rights are most difficult for you to surrender to Christ?

_____

_____

_____

_____

_____

BITE #9

To this you were called, because Christ suffered for you, leaving you an example, that you should follow in his steps.

1 Peter 2:21

If anyone had the **right** to demand just and fair treatment, it was Jesus. Yet he willingly set aside his **rights** and allowed himself to be crucified for **our** sins. We are to follow Christ's example and surrender our rights to the authority of his **Lordship**.

Peter ends verse 21 by saying we should follow in Christ's steps. Compare "following in his steps" with asking "What would Jesus do?" in every area of your life. How are some ways you can do that tomorrow?

_____

_____

_____

_____

He committed no sin, and no deceit was found in his mouth.

1 Peter 2:22

Jesus was perfect, yet he allowed himself to live in human form and face the temptations we experience.

But even during the times he was tempted, he never sinned. How does it make you feel to realize that Jesus really does understand how you feel and what you're experiencing when you face temptation? How does this knowledge put a different spin on your tempting times?

_____

_____

_____

> When they hurled their insults at him, he did not retaliate; when he suffered, he made no threats. Instead, he entrusted himself to him who judges justly.
>
> 1 Peter 2:23

Peter continues to link the Old Testament with his letter to the new Christians. Check out Isaiah 53:7:

> He was oppressed and afflicted, yet he did not open his mouth; he was led like a lamb to the slaughter, and as a sheep before its shearers is silent, so he did not open his mouth.

When someone insults you, how do you usually react?

_____

_____

When you're threatened, how do you respond?

_____

_____

_____

_____

Grab your Bible and turn to Mark 15:30. What did Jesus' hecklers encourage him to do?

_____

_____

_____

_____

Jesus was not only tortured and crucified, but his trial was unfair, and the people who testified against him had been bribed to create lies about him. It may have been tempting to expose all the wrong that was happening, but Jesus endured it all because:

_____ a. He knew that only his perfect blood could pay the price for your sins. He willingly endured because of his love for God and his love for you.

_____ b. He was confused and didn't know what else to do.

_____ c. He knew that if he called down an army of angels from heaven, war would have broken out and people would have focused on choosing sides instead of the fact that he was dying for the sins of the world.

_____ d. He was frightened beyond description.

When you're unjustly accused or when people make fun of you or lie about you, instead of seeking retaliation, how can you learn to simply trust yourself to God, who really does have everything in control?

_____

_____

_____

_____

"He himself bore our sins" in his body on the cross, so that we might die to sins and live for righteousness; "by his wounds you have been healed."

1 Peter 2:24

According to the above verse, who can die to their sins, receive forgiveness, and live righteously?

_____ a. All who go to church.

_____ b. People who have money, make good grades, and are popular.

_____ c. All minorities.

_____ d. Anyone and everyone!

Have you truly **died** to your sinful nature? Let's read Galatians 2:20:

> I have been crucified with Christ and I no longer live, but Christ lives in me.

What does the above verse have to say about dying to your sinful nature?

_____

_____

_____

When we allow Jesus to control our lives, and we live in surrender to his authority, we "die" to our rights, calling our own shots, and having our own way. We are **free** from sin's hold on our lives. We no longer have to be slaves to a sinful nature, but we can live in the **power** of the Holy Spirit residing within us. Our goal, then, is not only to be dead to sin, but also to live for **righteousness**. Our desire as Christians is to live a holy life.

Grab your Bible and read Romans 6:11-13. Fill in the blanks.

We are to be dead to _____ and alive to _____. Instead of offering our bodies to _____, we're to offer ourselves to _____. We've been brought from _____ to _____!

(You can find the correct answers at the end of Bite #9.)

For "you were like sheep going astray,'" but now you have returned to the Shepherd and Overseer of your souls.

1 Peter 2:25

Once again, Peter echoes the Old Testament in his letter to the Christians. Let's take a peek at Isaiah 53:6:

We all, like sheep, have gone astray, each of us has turned to his own way; and the Lord has laid on him the iniquity of us all.

Throughout the Bible, God is referred to as our Shepherd. List the qualities of a good shepherd:

_____

_____

_____

_____

God's children are often referred to as sheep. What are some characteristics of sheep?

_____

_____

_____

_____

_____

All sheep need a shepherd. Sheep aren't terribly intelligent. They don't even know when they're full and will continue eating to the point of endangering their lives! That's why a **good shepherd** will make them lie down after they eat. By lying flat on the ground, their **digestive systems** have a chance to digest the grass they've eaten.

What are some similarities between people and sheep?

_____

_____

_____

_____

_____

Take a moment to write an email to Christ thanking him for being your shepherd and tenderly caring for you as a shepherd cares for his sheep.

(Answers to the fill-in-the-blank Romans 6:11-13 section on p. 133: sin, God, sin, God, death, life.)

BITE #10

Grab a Friend

You just finished the second chapter of 1 Peter. Way to go! Now grab a friend and discuss the following questions together.

@ How have I declared God's praises this week?

@ Is there an area of my life in which I "rejected the Cornerstone" and his authority this past week?

@ Share with a friend what you learned about the Old Testament.

@ In what ways did I demonstrate faith in the Good Shepherd this week during my times of trial?

@ Practice giving your testimony to a friend.

Memorize It!

Try to memorize this verse with your friend and say it to each other the next time you get together:

> But you are a chosen people, a royal priesthood, a holy nation, God's special possession, that you may declare the praises of him who called you out of darkness into his wonderful light.
>
> 1 Peter 2:9

My Journal

Okay, Secret Power Girl, this is your space, so take advantage of it. You can do whatever you want here, but always try to include the following:

@ List your prayer requests. (Later, as God answers them, go back and record the date when God answered your prayer.)

@ Copy down any verse we studied in the previous chapter that you don't understand. Then let this be a reminder to ask your parents, Sunday school teacher, pastor, or youth leader about it.

@ Jot down what stood out the most from this chapter.

SECTION THREE

You Go, Girl!

1 Peter 3:1-22

BITE #1

> Wives, in the same way submit yourselves to your own husbands so that, if any of them do not believe the word, they may be won over without words by the behavior of their wives, when they see the purity and reverence of your lives.
>
> 1 Peter 3:1-2

In the previous chapter, Peter admonished the believers to submit to **governmental** authority. Imagine the chaos if no one obeyed the laws of the land! Now, he's encouraging **wives** to submit to their husbands. Just as we need order within the government, on our streets, and in schools, we also need order inside the **home**.

Peter isn't down on women; he's simply echoing the order God created for the home. He's not telling women to accept abuse or to disobey God.

This particular verse sounds as though Peter is talking to Christian women married to **nonbelievers**. He's not encouraging women to marry non-Christians, but for those who had already married—and the woman became a Christian later, while the husband didn't—he's saying a woman can **witness** to her husband by her gentle, respectful **behavior**.

Why is it important to marry someone who shares your faith?

_____

_____

_____

List eight qualities or characteristics you want in your future husband.

1._____

2._____

3._____

4. _____

5. _____

6. _____

7. _____

8. _____

How important is it that you marry someone who shares your faith? Is that on your list?

_____

_____

_____

Check out 2 Corinthians 6:14:

Do not be yoked together with unbelievers. For what do righteousness and wickedness have in common? Or what fellowship can light have with darkness?

What struggles will a married couple have in the following situations if they are unequally yoked (one is a Christian and the other isn't)?

• Going to church: _____

_____

- Studying the Bible together: _____

    _____

- Interpreting the Bible:_____

    _____

- Growing together spiritually:_____

    _____

How can sin separate a husband and wife?

_____

_____

_____

Your beauty should not come from outward adornment, such as elaborate hairstyles and the wearing of gold jewelry or fine clothes.

1 Peter 3:3

The Christian women in Peter's day weren't much different from Christian women today. They wanted to be **attractive**. That's a normal desire, and there's nothing wrong with that desire unless it becomes **unbalanced**.

Peter **isn't** telling women to cease taking care of themselves or to stop styling their **hair**. When we take the time to groom ourselves, and when we make good hygiene a daily part of our lives, we naturally feel better about ourselves.

It's okay to want to look our best—and we can do that with color, style, and fashion. But when we begin obsessing about outer appearance, we've become unbalanced. True beauty isn't comprised of our clothes or how we do our hair. True beauty...

_____ a. is something only celebrities possess (because they have the money to hire makeup artists and fashion consultants).

_____ b. comes from within.

_____ c. is displayed only by wearing the latest name brands.

_____ d. is found only in fairy tales.

Do you struggle with not feeling good enough, pretty enough, skinny enough, or cool enough? If so, you're not seeing yourself as Christ sees you. He made you in his image. Since he is perfect, what does this say about how he created you?

We often get messages about our appearance from the media (TV, magazines, movies, billboards), and the media is lying! Whenever you see a beautiful girl on the cover of a magazine, you can know for a fact that she doesn't actually look like that!

She has spent hours in a chair with professional makeup artists, hairstylists, and clothing stylists. Most of the time, a model will wear a size too small for her and an assistant will simply use huge pieces of thick tape to hold together the back of the dress, because it's too tight to be fastened together. But the public never sees that.

We see a bronzed goddess supermodel. We don't see the hours spent on spray tan before the photograph was taken. We see perfectly shaped, whitened teeth. We don't see the guy at the computer who has removed the yellowish color from the teeth and has straightened them.

We admire flawless skin. But we forget that the zits, wrinkles, and lines have been removed by Photoshop.

DON'T BELIEVE what you see! It's all a lie. DO BELIEVE that God loves you beyond description and is totally crazy about you! You are his princess. When he made you, he stepped back and said, "Ohhhh. This is good! This is really really, really good!" He's proud of his creation—you!

Rather, it should be that of your inner self, the unfading beauty of a gentle and quiet spirit, which is of great worth in God's sight. (1 Peter 3:4)

List some qualities that help radiate beauty from the inside.

_____

_____

_____

_____

Instead of depending on our clothes, skin, and hair to make us beautiful, we should rely instead on our inner selves, which have been **transformed** by the Holy Spirit. Our outer appearance can complement our inner beauty, but it shouldn't take the place of it or become more important than our **inner beauty**.

List three people you know who exhibit true inner beauty.

1. _____

2. _____

3. _____

How does their inner beauty radiate through their outer appearance?

_____

_____

_____

_____

_____

BITE #2

For this is the way the holy women of the past who put their hope in God used to adorn themselves.

1 Peter 3:5

How can we develop inner beauty?

_____

_____

_____

_____

Deep beauty, as seen in the saintly women of old would be comprised of gentleness, kindness, hospitality, devotion, loyalty, and love. List some women in the Bible who displayed these qualities.

_____

_____

_____

_____

They submitted themselves to their own husbands, like Sarah, who obeyed Abraham and called him her lord.

1 Peter 3:5-6

These women were **submissive**. That doesn't mean they were puppets controlled by their husbands. Nor does it mean they were doormats to be **walked** on by men.

It **does** mean they understood the ladder of authority that God **established**. Let's use another verse that will help us understand this concept a little better.

Flip to Ephesians 6:1: "Children, obey your parents in the Lord, for this is right."

Notice we're **not** told we have to agree with all our parents say and do. Our parents are human and will make mistakes. Though God doesn't command us to agree with them, God **does** command that we **honor** them.

God has established a ladder of authority that looks like this:

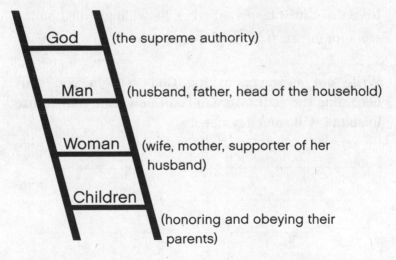

God   (the supreme authority)

Man   (husband, father, head of the household)

Woman   (wife, mother, supporter of her husband)

Children   (honoring and obeying their parents)

Notice that children are held **accountable** to their parents, and man is held accountable to Christ. This is the ladder of authority God has created for humankind.

Following this plan promotes unity and **harmony** in obedience to God.

Man is instructed to love his wife and children as **God** loves the **Church** (the Body of Christ). And someday man will have to answer to God as to how he loved his wife and children. When a **godly man** treats his wife with the honor, respect, and love that Christ lavishes on all of us, it's easy to honor or submit to him.

Again, Peter isn't telling women to turn into doormats. He's encouraging us to fit in with and **honor** the ladder of authority God has established.

Women are not to be slaves of their husbands. They are to be loving, **supportive** soul mates with their husbands, who in turn are to treat them with the **same kind of love** that Christ displayed when he willingly died on the cross for our sins.

Write out a prayer, asking God to help you start becoming the godly woman right now that your future husband will someday need.

_____

_____

_____

_____

_____

BITE #3

> They submitted themselves to their own husbands, like
> Sarah, who obeyed Abraham and called him her lord.
> You are her daughters if you do what is right and do not
> give way to fear.
>
> 1 Peter 3:5-6

Peter has chosen to **highlight** Sarah's obedience to her husband, Abraham. But there were also times of disobedience in Sarah and Abraham's marriage (Genesis 16:2, 6; 18:15). There were other times Sarah doubted Abraham and even made fun of him (Genesis 18:12). So why did Peter use Sarah as an example? She was considered the "mother of God's people," and she **did** display faithfulness to God and her husband.

Let's read the last part of 1 Peter 3:6 again:

> "You are her daughters if you do what is right and do not
> give way to fear."

We are encouraged to be like good daughters of Sarah. This is probably because...

_____ a. Sarah wanted more daughters.

_____ b. more mothers should be named Sarah.

_____ c. by being like good daughters of Sarah, we're also being heirs of God's promises to her and Abraham.

_____ d. more daughters should be named Sarah.

Peter says if women concentrate on doing what's **right**, they don't need to be fearful of their husbands. There are **two** ways we can look at this:

1. If a **godly** husband is treating his wife the way Christ would treat her, a woman doesn't need to be afraid to submit to that kind of love, and

2. Peter talks a lot about **persecution** in this letter. He's already told Christians not to be fearful of suffering. We can also carry that theme into this verse and assume he could be telling **Christian wives** not to be afraid of what could happen to them and their families, but place their trust completely in **Christ**.

Peter is **not** saying that wives should accept abuse from their husbands! **Any** woman who is living in an **abusive** situation needs to seek professional help.

> Husbands, in the same way be considerate as you live with your wives, and treat them with respect as the weaker partner and as heirs with you of the gracious gift of life, so that nothing will hinder your prayers.
>
> 1 Peter 3:7

Again, Peter isn't saying that wives are **slaves** of their husbands! He's saying a Christian wife should submit to the authority of her husband, but her husband in turn should be **consistently submissive** to the authority of Christ and treat his wife as Christ would.

When Peter admonishes husbands to be **considerate** of their wives, he's not merely suggesting kindness. Peter uses the word "considerate" to imply that a husband should be **in tune** with his wife's needs, dreams, goals, desires, likes, and dislikes. A godly husband who's this aware of his wife's needs and desires will obviously **complement** her life instead of making her miserable through demands and selfishness.

List your top ten "must-haves" for your future husband. This is different from the list of qualities you made earlier. These are things you won't negotiate or compromise.

1._____

2._____

3._____

4._____

5._____

6._____

7._____

8._____

9._____

10._____

When Peter refers to women as "the weaker sex," he's **not** demeaning women. And yes, there are some women who are physically stronger than some men. But God created man first, and **man** was created to be the stronger of the two sexes **physically**.

If we found the physically strongest woman and the physically strongest man in the world (same age bracket, same weight) and put them in a **weight-lifting contest** against each other, the male would win. He's simply built stronger than the woman. That's not saying women aren't strong; it's just that God created **one** sex physically stronger than the other.

But women are stronger than men in other areas. It's been said that women can handle pain better than men (because of what a woman goes through during childbirth). List some ways a woman's strengths can complement a man's weaker areas.

_____

_____

_____

_____

_____

The last thing Peter mentions in this verse is the prayer life of the husband. To have a strong, growing

relationship with Christ, we must also have positive relationships with those around us. Grab your Bible and turn to Matthew 5:23-24. What must be reconciled before we offer our gifts (praise, worship, tithe, etc.) to God?

_____

_____

_____

_____

_____

_____

Yes, God has called men to be the head of their homes—not in an abusive manner, but in a loving, caring way, as Jesus loves the church. If a husband uses this position God has placed him in to abuse, hurt, or ridicule his wife, his relationship with God will **suffer**.

During biblical times, women and children were considered **property**. In Peter's first letter to the Christians, he's encouraging godly men to **break that cycle**. Instead of treating women as property, Peter is teaching men to put their wives **first** and love them **unconditionally**.

When that occurs, it's easy to imagine that you could submit to his authority.

List 10 qualities you want your future husband to see in you.

1._____

2._____

3._____

4._____

5._____

6._____

7._____

8._____

9._____

10._____

Take a moment to pray for your future husband. This might seem weird, because you have no idea who he is. But you can still pray for him. Ask God to keep him pure, and pray that he'll become the strong spiritual leader you'll need in a husband.

BITE #4

Finally, all of you, be like-minded; be sympathetic, love one another, be compassionate and humble.

1 Peter 3:8

Define the following instructions.

Be like-minded:

_____

_____

_____

_____

Be sympathetic:

_____

_____

_____

_____

Love one another:

_____

_____

_____

_____

Be compassionate:

_____

_____

_____

_____

Be humble:

_____

_____

_____

_____

Now see if you can identify the following scenarios with the above phrases of how Peter tells us to act.

1. On her way home from school, Jennifer noticed a scraggly cat huddled next to a rain gutter. When she approached it with some leftovers from her sack lunch, the cat limped a few steps and then turned back to look at her. Jennifer spoke softly, approached the cat slowly, and cuddled it in her arms. She took it home, fed it milk, and posted an announcement in the "Lost and Found" section of her local newspaper.

Which of the following instructions was Jennifer displaying?

_____ a. Be like-minded.

_____ b. Be sympathetic.

_____ c. Love one another.

_____ d. Be compassionate.

_____ e. Be humble.

2. Nikki was in tears. "What's wrong, girl?" Mrs. Jamieson asked.

Nikki tried to blink back the tears, but she couldn't hide them from her favorite teacher. "I didn't make the cheerleading squad," she said.

"I'm sorry, Nikki. I really am."

"I don't understand, Mrs. Jamieson. I've been working on my stunts really hard, and I even took gymnastic lessons."

"Nikki, I know how you feel. When I was a sophomore, I thought making the varsity basketball team would be a breeze. I'd been playing since I was ten years old, and I was pretty good. But I was in a new high school, and the competition was really tough. Too tough. I didn't make it. But you know what? I worked really hard that summer, practiced about three hours a day, and I made the team my junior and senior years.

"I feel bad for you, Nikki. I'm really sorry you didn't make the squad. But I hope you'll keep trying and go for it again next year."

Which of the following instructions did Mrs. Jamieson display?

_____ a. Be like-minded.

_____ b. Be sympathetic.

_____ c. Love one another.

_____ d. Be compassionate.

_____ e. Be humble.

3. "Anyway," Ashley continued, "I just got a new violin. It's beautiful. My recital is next week, and I can't wait. My teacher says I'm one of the best he's ever taught."

"Wow! You *must* be good," Erica said. "How long have you been playing?"

"Almost a year," Ashley replied.

"That's terrific," Crystal chimed in.

"Hey, Crystal! Don't you play an instrument, too?" Erica asked.

"Well, yeah."

"What do you play?" Ashley asked.

"Well, I play the violin, too," Crystal said.

"Then how come you're not in the school orchestra like me?" Ashley asked.

"Oh, I remember now," Erica said. "You play in the state orchestra, don't you?"

"Yes," Crystal said quietly with a slight grin.

"So you must be *awesome!*" Erica continued.

Crystal didn't say anything.

"I mean, state orchestra is fantastic. Isn't that mainly comprised of adults?" Erica said.

"Well, there are a couple of other teens in the orchestra," Crystal said. "By the way, Ashley, I'd love to come to your recital next week. I'm so excited for you!"

Which of the following instructions did Crystal display?

_____ a. Be like-minded.

_____ b. Be sympathetic.

_____ c. Love one another.

_____ d. Be compassionate.

_____ e. Be humble.

4. Courtney was an only child and loved having her own bedroom. When she enrolled in college, however, she moved into a dorm room with two other girls as roommates. Alicia stayed up late and enjoyed inviting other girls into their room for popcorn and movies. Janet, on an athletic scholarship, went to bed early and got up early. She was extremely careful about her diet and routine. Courtney was used to going to bed whenever she wanted and having a quiet private place to study. The three girls, with different tastes and lifestyles, learned to get along and eventually became good friends in spite of their differences.

Which of the following instructions did Courtney display?

_____ a. Be like-minded.

_____ b. Be sympathetic.

_____ c. Love one another.

_____ d. Be compassionate.

_____ e. Be humble.

5. Jessica and Erin had been friends since third grade. They'd been in Girl Scouts together, learned to drive together, went shopping often, and became Christians during the same summer youth rally. They were extremely close friends.

Jessica's health began to fail during her senior year of high school. The doctor told her that one of her kidneys was failing, and she'd need a transplant. When Erin heard the news, her response was sure: "Let's see if I'm a match, Jessica," she said. "I love you like you're part of my own family."

Which of the following instructions did Erin display?

_____ a. Be like-minded.

_____ b. Be sympathetic.

_____ c. Love one another.

_____ d. Be compassionate.

_____ e. Be humble.

Check your answers below.

1. d. Be compassionate.

2. b. Be sympathetic.

3. e. Be humble.

4. a. Be like-minded.

5. c. Love one another.

Describe a time during the past month when you've displayed at least two of the above qualities.

_____

_____

_____

Ask God to help you develop these qualities as part of your lifestyle.

BITE #5

Do not repay evil with evil or insult with insult. On the contrary, repay evil with blessing, because to this you were called so that you may inherit a blessing.

1 Peter 3:9

God has a **high calling** on the lives of his children. God calls us to love as Christ loved. We're told in 1 Corinthians 13 (the "love" chapter of the Bible) that true love doesn't keep a record of wrongs. In other words, you **don't keep score** of the hurt others have caused you. This frees you to refrain from getting even.

Perhaps loving others doesn't come easily for you. The Holy Spirit can **transform** you into the loving disciple God is calling you to be. Peter himself didn't start out with a loving, tender personality. He was brash and impulsive, but he allowed God's Spirit to **break** him and **remake** him into the disciple Jesus knew Peter could become.

Grab your Bible and turn to John 13:6-9. Describe the scene: what's happening here?

_____

_____

_____

_____

What is Peter's response when Jesus starts to wash his feet?

_____

_____

_____

Jesus taught Peter humility—something Judas never learned. When you allow Jesus to teach you how to become **humble** (and this involves total surrender to his authority to break you and reshape you in his image), your concern with repaying evil and insults fades.

> For "Whoever would love life and see good days must keep their tongue from evil and their lips from deceitful speech. They must turn from evil and do good; they must seek peace and pursue it. For the eyes of the Lord are on the righteous and his ears are attentive to their prayer, but the face of the Lord is against those who do evil."
>
> 1 Peter 3:10-12

Peter again borrows from the **Old Testament** for this passage. You can read the same instructions from Psalm 34:12-16.

These Scriptures call the Christian to **action**. To keep our tongue from evil and our lips from deceitful speech doesn't mean we simply shut up and stand still. God calls us to love and affirm those around us. That requires **doing** something!

We chatted about 1 John 3:18 in Bite #10 (page 70) during our study of Peter's first chapter, but let's take another peek at this powerful verse: "Dear children, let us not love with words or speech but with actions and in truth."

To truly love as Jesus loved requires...

_____ a. an angel living inside my backpack.

_____ b. hypnosis.

_____ c. medication.

_____ d. action.

How have you loved in action this past week?

_____

_____

_____

Think of someone you find hard to get along with. How can you specifically love with action next week? What specifically will you do?

_____

_____

_____

BITE #6

Peter also tells us that we must "turn from evil and do good" and "seek peace and pursue it." These, too, require action! Jesus Christ was known as a loving, tender shepherd, but he was also known as an active radical acutely in tune with his Father's will. Jesus boldly lived in the center of God's will, which requires **action**!

And according to 1 Peter 3:12, what blessing do we receive when we actively follow God's will?

Who is going to harm you if you are eager to do good?
1 Peter 3:13

Who is more likely to be harmed, get in trouble, or be pursued by those in authority? (Mark your choice on the lines provided.)

_____ a. Emily shoplifts some makeup she wants.

_____ b. Danetta tries on a pair of jeans, likes the fit, and buys them.

_____ a. Jen doesn't understand the history assignment and asks her teacher for help after school.

_____ b. Lydia cheats on her history test.

_____ a. Caroline is late for work and breaks the speed limit.

_____ b. Brandi is careful to use her turn signals and obey the traffic laws.

Your choices on the above were probably extremely **easy**. They're obvious answers, aren't they? Usually we won't get in trouble or harmed if we're doing what's **right**. But we catch a different **spin** when we read Peter's next verse:

> But even if you should suffer for what is right, you are blessed. "Do not fear their threats; do not be frightened."
>
> 1 Peter 3:14

In the midst of his talk of love and peace, Peter keeps bringing up the subject of **suffering**, doesn't he? In fact, we could say that suffering is becoming a **theme** in his first letter to the early Christians. Though it seems we **shouldn't** be punished for doing what's right, we can't predict the actions of others. The world is full of those who hate Christians and seek to harm them.

The only thing we can be sure of is the fact that Jesus has promised to be with us in the midst of our pain and suffering. What does Jesus promise us in Matthew 28:20?

_____

_____

_____

_____

Peter tells us we're blessed if we suffer for doing what's right. How can that be?

_____ a. Peter had the flu when he wrote that verse.

_____ b. If we suffer for doing what's right, we're joining with Christ who also suffered, though he did no wrong.

_____ c. It's impossible.

_____ d. Because we get bonus points for doing what's right.

Can you identify a time when you noticed someone suffer for doing what was right?

_____

_____

_____

According to Matthew 5:10, who will be blessed?

_____

_____

_____

And what will be their reward?

_____

_____

_____

Read Matthew 5:11. You can be blessed when what happens?

_____

_____

_____

Now check out Matthew 5:12. What are we told to do in the midst of persecution?

_____

_____

_____

What is our blessing for rejoicing?

_____

_____

_____

We've read what Matthew and Peter encourage us to do in the midst of suffering. Let's see how the apostle James tells us to react to trials. Flip to James 1:2. How are we to respond to hard times?

_____

_____

_____

Why are we to respond this way? (See James 1:3.)

_____

_____

_____

How do you typically respond to trials?

_____

_____

_____

Take a moment to ask God to **rearrange** your thinking so you can begin to see problems and suffering in a new light.

BITE #7

But in your hearts revere Christ as Lord.

1 Peter 3:15)

What does it mean to make Christ LORD of your life?

_____

_____

_____

Have you done that?

_____

_____

_____

Keeping Jesus Lord of your life is a continuous process. It requires daily surrender to his will.

> Always be prepared to give an answer to everyone who asks you to give the reason for the hope that you have. But do this with gentleness and respect.
>
> 1 Peter 3:15

No one enjoys being around an obnoxious Christian— someone who's brash and always in your face. But the Christian who presents the Lord in gentle and kind ways often wins the respect of others around him or her. A strong disciple knows **what** she believes and **why**, and she's able to **articulate** her faith.

Are you able to explain why you're a Christian to those who question your faith? (If yes, what helped you become ready? If no, how can you prepare?)

_____

_____

_____

If we're truly trying to allow Christ to rule our hearts, we have a deep **knowledge** and a settled **peace** that he is in control of our world and our lives.

How does knowing that God is in control of the world and your life influence your perspective about what happens to you?

_____

_____

_____

But do this with gentleness and respect, keeping a clear conscience, so that those who speak maliciously against your good behavior in Christ may be ashamed of their slander.

1 Peter 3:15-16

Why is it important to keep a clear conscience?

_____

_____

_____

By telling the believers to keep a clear conscience, Peter is stressing that we mustn't simply look spiritually good on the outside, but on the inside as well. Our **minds** and **hearts** must be clean and match our outward good **actions**. He is saying that our lives should be characterized by integrity.

What is _integrity_?

_____ a. The name of a car.

_____ b. A brand of chewing gum.

_____ c. Pure motives and actions; dependable and trustworthy.

_____ d. A new soft drink.

Christians must realize that we will someday stand in front of the King of Kings and Lord of Lords who knows all and sees all. We should deeply desire, therefore, to live with personal integrity when people are watching—and when they aren't. Even when no one else is around to see our actions, we should live to please **God**.

But do this with gentleness and respect, keeping a clear conscience, so that those who speak maliciously against your good behavior in Christ may be ashamed of their slander.

1 Peter 3:15-16

Once again, Peter hints that Christians may experience suffering because of their faith in Christ. Disciples of Christ lived in a hostile world then, and they still do today. In parts of the world, Christians are being tortured **even as you read this sentence**. And it's not because they've done something wrong; it's simply because they've chosen to follow **Christ**.

Even when you don't face torture or death, you may still face strong opposition to your faith. People may make fun of you; they may ignore you; or they may **slander** you.

What does *slander* mean?

_____ a. To mix opposites.

_____ b. To speak evil of someone with the intent of destroying her reputation.

_____ c. To dance vigorously.

_____ d. To consume pizza excessively.

No one likes having things said about her that aren't true, especially when it's done to be deliberately hurtful.

It can be one of the more painful elements of many girls' lives—especially at school. But it's important to remember that God will walk with you, even in the midst of slander. If Jesus can die on a cross for our sin, don't think a little slander will keep him away!

Take a moment to write about how painful it is when someone slanders you, but remember also to thank God for being with you in the midst of that kind of pain.

_____

_____

_____

_____

The next time you're slandered (someone says something untrue, unkind, and mean about you), you may be tempted to get even and slander back. But with God's help, how will you respond instead?

_____

_____

_____

_____

BITE #8

> It is better, if it is God's will, to suffer for doing good than for doing evil.
>
> 1 Peter 3:17

It's **impossible** to keep people from saying bad things about you, but it **is** possible not to give them ammunition! In other words, if people slander or criticize you, don't let it be because you've harmed them or done something bad. That only adds **fuel** to the fire. It's always better, Peter reminds us, to suffer for doing something good than to suffer for doing something bad. We should **expect trouble** if we do something wrong; but unfortunately, many Christians have trouble when they're simply doing good.

> For Christ also suffered once for sins, the righteous for the unrighteous, to bring you to God.
>
> 1 Peter 3:18

Christ's death wasn't fair. He hadn't done anything wrong. He was perfect with no sin. Yet he willingly went to the cross so he could make the unrighteous righteous. Christ died for everyone, but unfortunately, not everyone accepts his free gift of salvation.

Why do you think so many people have not accepted Christ's forgiveness for their sins?

_____

_____

_____

_____

_____

> He was put to death in the body but made alive in the Spirit.
>
> 1 Peter 3:18

Someday we, too, will die, but as followers of Christ we have the assurance of **eternal life** with our Heavenly Father. In other words, we will be made **alive** again!

We get some "snapshots" of heaven in the book of Revelation, but we can't even imagine what it will be like. What are three things you're looking forward to in heaven?

1. _____

2. _____

3. _____

What are three questions you'll want to ask God once you're in heaven?

1. _____

2. _____

3. _____

He was put to death in the body but made alive in the Spirit. After being made alive he went and made proclamation to the imprisoned spirits—to those who were disobedient long ago when God waited patiently in the days of Noah while the ark was being built. In it only a few people, eight in all, were saved through water.

1 Peter 3:18-20

The exact meaning of these verses is **unclear**, and you'll find several different perspectives in a variety of commentaries. Some theologians believe that Christ's Spirit was in **Noah** and enabled him to preach to those around him before the flood. Others believe "the spirits in prison" refer to those who died **before** Christ and were held in a "prison" or a holding cell until Christ could come and preach to them.

We can be content to simply say, "We're not sure" about the exact meaning of the above passage, but we **can** be sure that salvation has been, and is being, preached through the ages.

We should strive to live with the strong faith of Noah.

Imagine yourself in his shoes. Some biblical scholars believe that up to this point in time, the world had not seen rain; the ground was watered by dew. So when God told Noah there would be a **flood**, he really had no conception of what that meant. **But he still trusted God!**

What if God said this to you: "I know you don't understand what **bufskap** is, but there's going to be a lot of bufskap! In fact, there will be so much bufskap that you'll **perish**—unless you build something big enough and high enough to keep you above the **bufskap**. Listen carefully, and I'll give you specific instructions on **what** to build and **how** to build it. If you follow my instructions and trust me, you'll be saved. But if you don't, you'll **die** in the bufskap."

How would you react?

_____

_____

_____

How would your friends, loved ones, and classmates react to your new building project?

_____

_____

_____

What would you say to those around you?

_____

_____

_____

Perhaps now you can relate in a small way to Noah. Write a prayer in the space provided, asking Christ to strengthen your faith so you can **accept** his ways without having to **understand** them.

BITE #9

And this water symbolizes baptism that now saves you also—not the removal of dirt from the body but the pledge of a clear conscience toward God.

1 Peter 3:21

Think back to Noah again. The water saved him by keeping him **afloat** during the flood, but the water also **destroyed** the unbelievers. We're not saved by **water**; we're saved by God's **grace**. But baptism is important to the believer because it's a testimony of God's salvation. As water washes dirt from our bodies, so Christ washes sin from our hearts. As we're **baptized** in water, we're demonstrating what Christ has done for us; we're testifying to others that he has cleansed us from sin.

Read about Jesus' baptism in Matthew 3:13-17. Who baptized Jesus?

_____

_____

What did God say after Jesus was baptized?

_____

_____

_____

Now grab your Bible and check out Ephesians 5:1. Who are we to imitate?

_____

_____

If **Jesus** sought baptism, we should take baptism seriously, too. Have you been baptized? If not, consider making an appointment with your pastor or youth leader to talk about getting baptized. How can public baptism help keep believers accountable to the Body of Christ?

> It saves you by the resurrection of Jesus Christ, who has gone into heaven and is at God's right hand—with angels, authorities and powers in submission to him.
>
> 1 Peter 3:21-22

It's not baptismal **water** that saves us; only God can transform us from within. But by being baptized, we are doing what Christ did. By becoming baptized, we're saying, "We **believe** your Word, Jesus. We **identify** with other believers who have also joined together to follow you. We **trust** your desire and power to save us."

Express in your own words why baptism is important.

_____

_____

_____

Have you been baptized?

_____ Yes   _____ No

If you haven't been baptized, will you talk with your parents and your pastor about being baptized? It's a great way to testify to other believers that you love God and are obeying him by being baptized. It's also symbolic of him cleansing you from sin and washing you clean.

Next, Peter reminds us that Christ is alive and well. According to the passage, where is Christ, and who is he with?

Peter tells us that angels, authorities, and powers are in **submission** to Christ. He is the King of all Kings! If we want to become all God desires for us to be, we too will live in submission to the authority of Christ.

BITE #10

Grab a Friend

Congratulations! You just finished the third chapter of 1 Peter. Now grab a friend and discuss the following questions together.

@ Peter instructs us to "be like-minded." What are specific ways I have done that this week?

@ Are there things I've participated in this week that would contribute to keeping me from having a clear conscience?

@ Can I explain why it's important to only date (and eventually marry) someone who shares my faith?

Memorize It!

Try to memorize this verse with your friend and say it to each other the next time you get together:

> Finally, all of you, be like-minded; be sympathetic, love one another, be compassionate and humble.
>
> 1 Peter 3:8

My Journal

Okay, Secret Power Girl, this is your space, so take advantage of it. You can do whatever you want here, but always try to include the following:

@ List your prayer requests. (Later, as God answers them, go back and record the date when God answered your prayer.)

@ Copy down any verse we studied in the previous chapter that you don't understand. Then let this be a reminder to ask your parents, Sunday school teacher, pastor, or youth leader about it.

@ Jot down what stood out the most from this chapter.

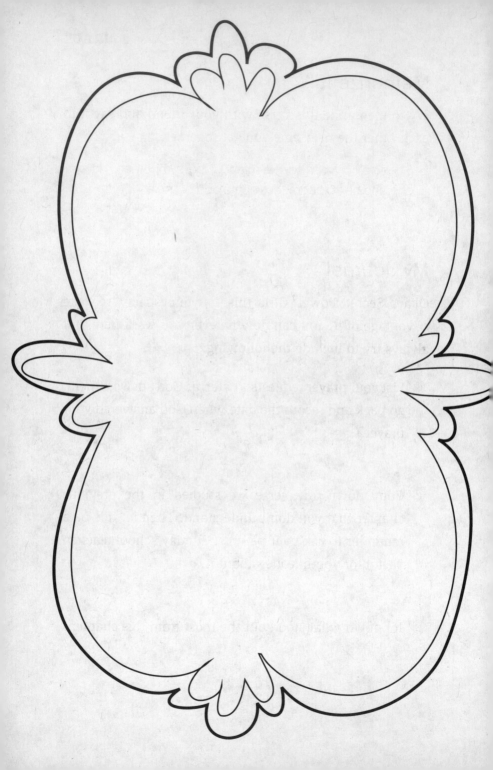

Keep Your Mind Clear

1 Peter 4: 1-19

BITE #1

Therefore, since Christ suffered in his body, arm yourselves also with the same attitude, because whoever suffers in the body is done with sin.

1 Peter 4:1

Describe a few of the most common physical pains in your life that you try to avoid. (Cutting yourself while shaving your legs, having the dentist fill a cavity, etc.)

_____

_____

It would be **impossible** to go through life without pain. Do you know someone who will do anything to avoid pain—even at the expense of her health? (For example, Sarah avoids the dentist because she's afraid of being hurt.)

Peter has already instructed believers to **rejoice** in their sufferings, to **identify with Christ** in their sufferings, and to suffer for doing **good**, not bad. But now he puts a different **spin** on suffering. He tells us that suffering helps us to be "done with sin."

This doesn't mean that if we suffer for Christ's sake, we're **exempt** from sinning. We're still human, and we can still sin—even in the midst of suffering. But when someone is persecuted for her faith in Christ, her true self—her true values and priorities—rise to the surface.

With our priorities **clearly** in view, sin doesn't seem as enticing. When our lives are at stake, sinful pleasures aren't so important anymore.

"Arm yourselves also with the same attitude..." What does it mean to "arm yourself"?

_____

_____

_____

_____

_____

"The same attitude" refers to Christ's attitude when he suffered. It's not often that we're told to "get an attitude," but Peter is telling us just that! We are to have the same attitude as Christ. What attitude did he have in the midst of suffering that we need to imitate?

_____

_____

_____

Imitating Christ's attitude, of course, is a good thing! What are some not-so-good attitudes you struggle with?

_____

_____

_____

Let's do an attitude check by taking this quiz. What would your actions and attitude be in the following situations?

1. Olivia has been your best friend since elementary school, and you always sit together at lunchtime. Today, however, you see her sitting with a new girl when you walk into the cafeteria. You

    _____ a. Ignore her.

    _____ b. Ask if you can sit with both of them and introduce yourself to the new girl.

_____ c. Tell her off in front of the new girl.

_____ d. Look for a new best friend.

2. Glen is known as the school bully. Your paths usually don't cross, but today he overheard you invite someone to church. At lunchtime, he takes your food tray from you and dumps it all over your front. He says, "I don't like church girls," and walks away. You

_____ a. Scream insults at him as he's leaving.

_____ b. Make it a point to find him later and say, "It's okay that you don't like church girls, but God is way bigger than church. I invite you to give him a chance."

_____ c. Start tweeting nasty things about Glen.

_____ d. Toss ice cream in his face the following day.

3. In one of your classes, you're assigned to give a persuasive speech. You speak against abortion—hoping to help your classmates see that it's wrong. Not only do the students disagree with you, but the teacher downplays your research and claims that you've allowed your religious beliefs to influence everything you said. You

_____ a. Storm out of class.

_____ b. Speak up and say, "Yes, my faith influences everything I do—just as your believe system has influenced how you've reacted to my speech. But my faith can't change the facts of the research I've presented. Facts are facts.

_____ c. Approach the teacher after class and tell him you don't really believe abortion is wrong.

_____ d. Tell the teacher he doesn't know what he's talking about.

4. Your school is having a Sadie Hawkins banquet—the girls ask the guys. You ask Jason, a friend from church, if he'll go with you. He agrees. But a week before the banquet, you see the most popular girl at school talking with him in the hallway. That evening Jason texts you saying he can't take you because his plans have changed. You

_____ a. Go to the banquet with some girlfriends and see Jason with _her_. You waste no time in screaming, "You're a jerk!" to him and his date.

_____ b. Go to the banquet with some girlfriends. When you see Jason with her, you simply smile and say, "Hi, Jason."

_____ c. Refuse to attend the banquet. You know

who Jason is going with. You stay home and put nasty things on Facebook about the two of them.

_____ d. Approach him the next day and call him a two-timing liar.

In the above scenarios, the B response is the attitude Christ would have. How'd you do? It's easy to let our own reactions get in the way of having Christ's attitude, isn't it? That's why we need his help. Make it a habit of daily asking Christ to give you his attitude and to empower you to reflect him.

> As a result, they do not live the rest of their earthly lives for evil human desires, but rather for the will of God.
>
> 1 Peter 4:2

Suffering for Christ and maintaining our faith in him helps **solidify** our submission to his will. The more we identify with Christ in his suffering, the more we're **drawn** to him. Sinful pleasures have less and less appeal to us. Knowing and doing God's will becomes the driving **force** of our lives.

Do you struggle with anything that keeps obedience to God from being the driving force in **your** life?

BITE #2

For you have spent enough time in the past doing what pagans choose to do—living in debauchery, lust, drunkenness, orgies, carousing and detestable idolatry.

1 Peter 4:3

No matter how old you were when you became a Christian, you have already spent enough time in sin. If you became a Christian at age 8 or at age 18, your past is your past. **Don't go back** to the attitudes, habits, and lifestyle you had before you gave your life to Christ. He has done a **brand new** work in you. Now continue walking with him so he can **finish** the work he's started in your life!

You may have a simple testimony; you may have a colorful testimony. But everyone has a testimony! Perhaps you were self-centered, selfish, or you gossiped. What are some of the things you used to do (or attitudes that you used to have) that you no longer do (or have) now that you're a Christian?

_____

_____

_____

_____

_____

_____

They are suprised that you do not join them in their reckless, wild living, and they heap abuse on you.

1 Peter 4:4

What kinds of reactions do your non-Christian friends give when you refuse to do things with them that you know are wrong?

_____

_____

_____

Identify a time when you were made fun of because of your morals.

_____

_____

_____

If you've been criticized for not joining in with others when they do things Christ doesn't want you to do, congratulations! That proves you're taking a stand. It means those around you notice the difference in your life. Peter is telling the believers to expect abuse for refusing to join sinners in their lifestyle.

But they will have to give account to him who is ready to judge the living and the dead.

1 Peter 4:5

Someday we'll all face the judgment of Christ. Grab your Bible and turn to Romans 14:11. Who will someday bow before God?

_____

_____

Who will someday confess that Jesus Christ is Lord?

_____

_____

We will all be held **accountable** for the way we lived our lives.

For this is the reason the gospel was preached even to those who are now dead, so that they might be judged according to human standards in regard to the body, but live according to God in regard to the spirit.

1 Peter 4:6

To follow God—or not to follow God. This is a **decision** that affects people of all **centuries**. Even before Christ walked the earth, God was speaking through prophets. And Jesus has promised not to return for his people until the entire world has heard the plan of salvation.

List as many ways as you can think of that the gospel of Christ is being proclaimed right now throughout the world.

_____

_____

_____

_____

_____

_____

_____

_____

BITE #3

The end of all things is near. Therefore be alert and of sober mind so that you may pray.

1 Peter 4:7

No one knows the exact time or date that Christ will return, but we're told to live expectantly. If you knew for a fact that Christ was returning in two days, what would you do?

_____

_____

_____

Why should we live expectantly as though Christ is returning tomorrow?

_____

_____

_____

Grab your Bible and read 1 Thessalonians 5:2-3. What does this say about Christ's return?

_____

_____

_____

Let's take another look at 1 Peter 4:7: "The end of all things is near. Therefore be alert and of sober mind so that you may pray." Define the opposite of clear-minded.

_____

_____

_____

Define the opposite of self-controlled.

_____

_____

_____

It's difficult to keep a clear head when we're being persecuted, and it's tough to be self-controlled when we're criticized. But if we intently focus our attention on Christ's return, it helps us keep a godly mind-set; we're able to live with a clear head and self-control. Getting our focus away from Christ's coming can easily contribute to revenge, selfishness, and blurred thinking.

> Above all, love each other deeply, because love covers over a multitude of sins.
>
> 1 Peter 4:8

Peter has talked quite a bit about suffering in his first letter to the Christians. He knew that "to love each other deeply" would help the believers endure suffering. How has someone's deep love for you helped you endure a tough time?

_____

_____

_____

Perhaps you've heard the phrase, "No Christian is an island." What do you think that means?

_____ a. We don't all know how to swim.

_____ b. No Christian should live on an island.

_____ c. We should all swim more.

_____ d. No Christian should try to make it alone; we all need support from the body of Christ.

When Peter tells us that "love covers over a multitude of sins," he wasn't saying that love **ignores** or excuses sin. Jesus loves us so much he **died** for us, yet he has never ignored or **excused** sin.

When he confronted the woman caught in adultery, he didn't make excuses: "Well, you didn't realize what you were doing; it's okay." He never flinched at calling sin "sin."

Yet Peter says, "love covers over a multitude of sin." Again, he's **instructing** believers to live in harmony, to get along, and to love deeply. When we love as Jesus loved, we can **forgive** others of their sins, no matter how badly they've hurt us. This kind of love "covers over" the sins of others. Remember that **true love** (according to 1 Corinthians 13) doesn't hold grudges!

When we hesitate to forgive those who have hurt us, we hinder our relationship with Christ. List any sins of others you're struggling to forgive.

_____

_____

_____

_____

How would genuine love affect your response to the following situations?

The guy you secretly like asks out your friend.

_____

_____

_____

You loaned your favorite hoodie to a friend, and she lost it.

_____

_____

_____

You've had your eye on a specific dress for a month. You've been saving until you have enough money to purchase it for the spring banquet. Your friend buys it before you have a chance to finish saving.

_____

_____

_____

_____

_____

BITE #4

Offer hospitality to one another without grumbling.

1 Peter 4:9

Most young people want to have friends over, throw parties, and be hospitable. In fact, they look forward to it! What do you think are some reasons hospitality becomes harder as we get older? (Circle all that apply.)

happy   loving others   expensive

jokes

the house that needs painting   takes too much energy   poor health

weather

too much work   the dog needs a walk

guests stay too long   people eat too much

Grab your Bible and turn to Hebrews 13:2. What has happened when some people have been hospitable to strangers?

_____

_____

_____

Describe the most recent time you were hospitable.

_____

_____

_____

> Each of you should use whatever gift you have received
> to serve others, as faithful stewards of God's grace in its
> various forms.
>
> 1 Peter 4:10

For information on discovering your **spiritual gifts,** get the first book in the Secret Power series: _Secret Power for Girls._

Every Christian has received at least one spiritual **gift** from God. When we dedicate our gifts to God, the Giver, they can be used to bring **glory** to God. This is what makes the body of Christ harmonious and unified. Some people teach; some help financially; some organize; others sing. When **everyone** uses his or her gift, it makes a healthy church.

List three things you love to do and do well.

1._____

2._____

3._____

What do you think your spiritual gifts might be?

_____

_____

_____

_____

> If anyone speaks, they should do so as one who speaks the very words of God. If anyone serves, they should do so with the strength God provides, so that in all things God may be praised through Jesus Christ. To him be the glory and the power for ever and ever. Amen.
>
> 1 Peter 4:11

We may be tempted to use our special gifts any way we please or simply for our own enjoyment. This would be **misusing** what God has blessed us with. Our gifts are to be used to **edify** (build up) the Church and to glorify Christ. How have you edified the Church with your special gifts?

Flip to Romans 12:6-8, 1 Corinthians 12:8-11, and Ephesians 4:11-13, and list as many special gifts as you can find.

God has given Christ power and authority over all creation forever. It's only through **Jesus** that we can even have a relationship with **God**.

Amen is another way of saying, "that's it," or "so be it."

BITE #5

> Dear friends, do not be surprised at the fiery ordeal that has come on you to test you, as though something strange were happening to you.
>
> 1 Peter 4:12

Peter refers to the Christians he's writing to as "dear friends." This stresses the importance of **unity** among those in the church, even though he hadn't met most of them. Non-Christians are sometimes **surprised** at the behavior of Christians. They don't understand how we can respond to criticism with love, or how we can trust a God we can't see.

But Peter is reminding the believers once again not to be surprised at the behavior of non-Christians who inflict suffering on God's followers. Don't be caught off guard when you're criticized for your faith in Jesus.

Let's take a look at John 15:18: "If the world hates you, keep in mind that it hated me first."

Who's talking in the above verse?

_____

_____

_____

_____

Why should Christians expect to be hated or criticized by nonbelievers?

_____

_____

_____

_____

But inasmuch as you participate in the sufferings of Christ, so that you may be overjoyed when his glory is revealed.

1 Peter 4:13

Instead of being confused, surprised, bewildered, or caught off guard by trials, Peter tells the believers to **rejoice**! When we suffer for our faith, it proves we're true followers of Christ. Check out John 15:20: "If they persecuted me, they will persecute you also."

Write down the various emotions you have felt and expressed when you suffered for your faith.

_____

_____

_____

If you are insulted because of the name of Christ, you are blessed, for the Spirit of glory and of God rests on you.

1 Peter 4:14

List some people in history—or whom you know personally—who have been insulted because of their faith in Christ.

_____

_____

_____

_____

Christ has promised to send his Spirit to strengthen those who are insulted for their faith. How does this make you feel?

_____

_____

_____

_____

If you suffer, it should not be as a murderer or thief or any other kind of criminal, or even as a meddler. However, if you suffer as a Christian, do not be ashamed, but praise God that you bear that name.

1 Peter 4:15-16

Peter again reinforces the fact that Christians should

expect suffering, but the only time we're **blessed** for suffering is when we're suffering for our **faith**. We're not blessed when we suffer for doing something wrong. For example, if you steal something and suffer the consequences, that's expected. You won't be blessed for the suffering you've endured.

Peter also tells us to praise God that we bear the name of "**Christian**." Describe a time when you were proud of your faith and knew God was proud of you as well.

BITE #6

For it is time for judgment to begin with the family of God; and if it begins with us, what will the outcome be for those who do not obey the gospel of God?

1 Peter 4:17

Peter wanted to make sure the believers understood that **everyone** will be judged. Both the righteous and the unrighteous will bow before God and confess that Christ is Lord. For believers who **obey** God, this won't be a frightening time; it will be a time of **praise.** But for those who have **refused** to accept him as Savior, the judgment will be a time of grief, fright, and revelation. They will be **separated** from Christ forever and will spend eternity in hell.

Grab your Bible and read 2 Peter 2:4. Who went to hell?

_____

_____

_____

Many people say, "How can a God of love send anyone to hell?" We need to remember that God doesn't want anyone to go to hell. If someone goes to hell, it's because she has rejected God, and in doing so, she's **chosen** to spend eternity in hell.

And "if it is hard for the righteous to be saved, what will become of the ungodly and the sinner?"

1 Peter 4:18

Peter again brings in the Old Testament through this verse. Grab your Bible and read Proverbs 11:31. What will the sinner receive?

_____

_____

_____

When Peter says "if it is hard for the righteous to be saved," he's talking about the hard road of **suffering** believers face. "To be saved" doesn't mean God has a difficult time forgiving us; it refers to the whole process of salvation, emphasizing **perseverance** to the end.

What's one of the toughest things you've encountered since placing your faith in Christ?

_____

_____

_____

Though the righteous experience suffering on earth, we can't imagine how much greater eternal suffering will be in hell for those who aren't Christians. List

three people you know who haven't accepted Christ as their personal Savior.

1._____

2._____

3._____

Knowing that these people will spend eternity in hell unless they come to Christ, what can you do this week to remind them of God's immeasurable love?

> So then, those who suffer according to God's will should commit themselves to their faithful Creator and continue to do good.
>
> 1 Peter 4:19

"Suffer[ing] according to God's will" means that God is in control. God doesn't **cause** us to suffer, but he **does** allow it, just as he allowed Jesus to suffer. We don't always understand why things happen as they do; we can't understand the **mind** of God. But we can rest in the assurance that God loves us **completely** and has promised to be with us **in the midst of** our suffering.

If we place 100 percent of our trust in Christ, what is there to fear? Check out 1 John 4:4. Who's greater than Satan?

BITE #7

Grab a Friend

You just finished the fourth chapter of 1 Peter. Way to go! Now grab a friend and discuss the following questions together.

@ How have I used my spiritual gifts this week?

@ Have I reverted back to behavior or habits this week that I practiced before I became a Christian? If so, seek forgiveness now. If not, thank God with your friend for helping you remain consistent in your relationship with Christ.

@ How have I identified with Christ this week?

@ When did I display great attitudes this week? When did I display not-so-great attitudes?

Memorize It!

Try to memorize this verse with your friend and say it to each other the next time you get together:

> Each of you should use whatever gift you have received to serve others, as faithful stewards of God's grace in its various forms.
>
> 1 Peter 4:10

My Journal

Okay, Secret Power Girl, this is your space, so take advantage of it. You can do whatever you want here, but always try to include the following:

@ List your prayer requests. (Later, as God answers them, go back and record the date when God answered your prayer.)

@ Copy down any verse we studied in the previous chapter that you don't understand. Then let this be a reminder to ask your parents, Sunday school teacher, pastor, or youth leader about it.

@ Jot down what stood out the most from this chapter.

Hangin' Wit' da Sheep

1 Peter 5:1-14

BITE #1

> To the elders among you, I appeal as a fellow elder and
> a witness of Christ's sufferings who also will share in the
> glory to be revealed.
>
> 1 Peter 5:1

Peter had a **lot** to his credit: He was one of the 12 disciples
Jesus personally selected to follow him. He was one of the
three closest people to Christ (John and James were the
other two). He was called **"The Rock"** by Jesus himself
and told that the **Church** would be built on him. He saw

and spoke with Jesus after the resurrection. He **preached** at Pentecost when the believers first felt the power of the Holy Spirit within them, and he was a strong leader in early church growth. He could've easily **boasted** about these accomplishments, but he knew better.

This is called humility. Write down the name of someone you know who has accomplished a lot and could be proud but has chosen instead to remain humble.

Instead, he placed himself on the **same level** as the elders of this church. Peter didn't come off sounding superior; he was determined to promote **unity** and wanted to appear one with them.

Who were the elders?

_____ a. People who were really, really old but still hung out at church.

_____ b. Anyone in the church who had lots of wrinkles.

_____ c. Those who gave the most money.

_____ d. Those in leadership positions in the church who provided discipline, supervision, protection, instruction, and direction for the other believers.

Be shepherds of God's flock that is under your care, watching over them—not because you must, but because you are willing, as God wants you to be; not pursuing dishonest gain, but eager to serve; not lording it over those entrusted to you, but being examples to the flock.

1 Peter 5:2-3

Peter is passing along the instructions Christ had given him in John 21:15-18. Turn to that passage now and write down what Christ specifically told Peter to do (and even repeated it three times!).

Who are the sheep?

_____

_____

_____

Christ isn't telling Peter to take actual food to real animals. Rather he's instructing Peter to feed the Christians God's Word. Why do we grow spiritually when we read the Bible and listen to Christian teaching?

Genuine service for God comes from true love rather than obligation. Hopefully, you do God's will because you want to, not because you're supposed to. Peter encourages the believers to be examples to other Christians. In other words: We need to "feed sheep," too! To whom and how can you be an example?

_____

_____

_____

_____

And when the Chief Shepherd appears, you will receive
the crown of glory that will never fade away.

1 Peter 5:4

**The "crown of glory" serves as a motivator for Christian
service. In what ways are you personally involved in
Christian service?**

_____

_____

_____

**Grab your Bible and turn to 1 Corinthians 9:24. How
many people win the race?**

_____

_____

_____

**Now read 1 Corinthians 9:25. What happens to the
prize an athlete wins?**

_____

_____

_____

What happens to the prize—or crown—that we will someday receive?

_____

_____

_____

Check out 1 Corinthians 9:26. How should we *not* run the race?

_____

_____

_____

Read 1 Corinthians 9:27. How serious is Paul about training and running the race to win?

_____

_____

_____

The race is compared to our Christian walk. How serious are you about your Christian race?

_____

_____

_____

What's your training program? In other words, what are you doing to deepen your relationship with Christ?

_____

_____

_____

Let's look at 1 Peter 5:4 again:

And when the Chief Shepherd appears, you will receive the crown of glory that will never fade away.

Peter begins this verse with the word "and" which ties it into the verse before this one in which he tells believers to "feed sheep." If we want the crown of glory, we must involve ourselves in Christian **work**. We need to be **doing** things for the Kingdom. Many people don't want to talk about "doing things for Christ," because they focus on grace over works. While it's true that **salvation** comes only through God's grace, the Bible is clear that God also expects us to do good **works**. So Peter is using the "crown of glory" to **motivate** us to do all we can for Christ and each other while here on earth.

BITE #2

In the same way, you who are younger, submit yourselves
to your elders. All of you, clothe yourselves with humility
toward one another, because, "God opposes the proud
but shows favor to the humble."

1 Peter 5:5

**In 1 Peter 3, the apostle gives us God's best plan
for relationships within the home: God as the head,
followed by men, women, and children. Here, he gives
God's best plan for relationships within the church.
List three elders in your own church you truly respect,
and explain how you can see the fingerprints of God
on their lives.**

1. _____

_____

_____

2. _____

_____

_____

3. _____

_____

_____

In the last portion of verse five, Peter again brings in the Old Testament. Grab your Bible and turn to Proverbs 3:34. Whom does God mock?

_____

_____

_____

To whom does God give grace?

_____

_____

_____

> Humble yourselves, therefore, under God's mighty hand, that he may lift you up in due time.
>
> 1 Peter 5:6

Peter uses the word "therefore" to connect this Scripture to the one before it. In other words, we could say, "*Because* God opposes the proud but gives grace to the humble, start humbling yourself under God's mighty hand."

Humility doesn't come naturally to most people. We have to **work** at it. We have to make a conscious decision to be humble. When we humble ourselves under God's mighty hand, we're living in **submission** to God. Guess what—that's exactly where every Christian should live!

Peter borrows the phrase "God's mighty hand" from the

Old Testament. It's often used to describe God's **power**. Let's read Psalm 32:4.

> For day and night your hand was heavy on me; my strength was sapped as in the heat of summer.

According to the above verse, how is God's hand described?

_____

_____

_____

Does it make sense, then, that Peter tells us to be **submissive** under God's hand? Why would we want to **fight** the strength, wisdom, and power of the Creator of the universe?

For another Old Testament example of God's **hand**, check out Job 30:21: "You turn on me ruthlessly; with the might of your hand you attack me."

Of course, God never ignores our cries, but Job felt as though God wasn't listening. Describe a time when you felt God was ignoring you.

_____

_____

_____

The next time you feel God is ignoring you, remind yourself of two **truths:**

#1: *You can't trust your feelings.* Our feelings are often as high and low as a roller coaster. The heart will often deceive us. But you **can** trust God. Always!

#2: *God never ignores you!* "For he who avenges blood remembers; he does not ignore the cry of the afflicted" (Psalm 9:12). Memorize that verse.

BITE #3

Cast all your anxiety on him because he cares for you.
                                            1 Peter 5:7

How much of your problems or anxiety does Peter tell you to give Christ?

_____ About ten percent.

_____ Thirty-eight percent.

_____ One week's worth.

_____ ALL of it.

According to the above verse, why should you cast your anxiety on God?

_____

_____

_____

What does it mean to cast your anxiety on God?

_____

_____

_____

What are you anxious about that you need to cast on God right now?

_____

_____

_____

> Be alert and of sober mind. Your enemy the devil prowls around like a roaring lion looking for someone to devour.
>
> 1 Peter 5:8

To be "alert and of sober mind" requires **action**. We can't be sober minded and alert while we're standing **idle** or flat-footed. We need to be **on our toes** spiritually! In other words, Christians need to live on the **defense** against Satan's attacks.

Maybe you've heard the coach during a basketball game shouting to his team, "Wake up, defense!" It's his way of telling his players to be more **alert** and **attentive**. He's commanding them to be on the defensive against the **opponent**.

In the spiritual realm, who is your opponent?

_____ a. Anyone who doesn't attend my church.

_____ b. Satan.

_____ c. Anyone who crosses me.

_____ d. Anyone who doesn't want to sit next to me at lunch.

Satan is paralleled to a roaring **lion** looking for a victim. Lions don't seek strong prey; they look for weak animals that stand alone or are **sleeping**. Satan works the same way. If you're spiritually **alert** and living on the **defense**, Satan will have a much harder time attacking you. If you've fallen asleep spiritually, though, you're an easy victim!

The first step in falling asleep spiritually is to become comfortable with things in our lives that God doesn't want us accustomed to. In what areas of your life do you tend to "fall asleep?"

_____

_____

_____

Go ahead and commit the above areas to God through a prayer right now. It can be a spoken prayer, or you may want to write a prayer in the space below.

_____

_____

_____

BITE #4

Resist him, standing firm in the faith, because you know that the family of believers throughout the world is undergoing the same kind of sufferings.

1 Peter 5:9

One way to resist Satan is to stay intently focused on Christ. The more we saturate our lives with him, the easier it is to resist the enemy. Grab your Bible and turn to James 4:7. According to this verse, what's the benefit of resisting Satan?

_____

_____

_____

Now read James 4:8. What happens when you draw near to God?

_____

_____

_____

Let's take another look at 1 Peter 5:9.

Resist him, standing firm in the faith, because you know that the family of believers throughout the world is undergoing the same kind of sufferings.

When we're in the midst of suffering, it's easy to focus on ourselves: **our** hurt, **our** trial, **our** specific situations. Peter is telling us to get our eyes off ourselves and remember that we're not the only ones suffering!

How does it make you feel to know that you're not alone in your suffering—that other Christians know exactly what you're going through—because they're also experiencing it?

Stop right now and write a prayer for Christians around the world who are suffering.

_____

_____

_____

And the God of all grace, who called you to his eternal glory in Christ, after you have suffered a little while, will himself restore you and make you strong, firm and steadfast.

1 Peter 5:10

This verse helps us get a **wider** perspective. Instead of simply focusing on the tough times we're experiencing, we're called instead to remember our **calling**. God has a high calling on the lives of his children; it's an **eternal** calling. When we think about our real lives in eternity, it forces us to remember that what we're experiencing now is **temporary**!

What's the worst thing you've experienced in the past month?

_____

_____

_____

When you place that next to your eternal life in heaven, does it give you a different perspective on your trials?

_____

_____

_____

Then Peter reminds us that we have a promise! According to the above verse, what will happen after we've suffered a little while?

_____

_____

_____

Let's take another look at the same verse from The Living Bible:

> After you have suffered a little while, our God, who is full of kindness through Christ, will give you his eternal glory. He personally will come and pick you up, and set you firmly in place, and make you stronger than ever.

We're reminded from this verse that God is full of...

_____a. color.

_____ b. kindness.

_____ c. emails.

_____ d. laughter.

We're also reminded that God is personally interested and involved in everything we experience. What does this verse say that God will do after we have suffered a little while?

_____

_____

_____

How does this change your perspective on any trials you may experience?

_____

_____

_____

To him be the power for ever and ever. Amen.

1 Peter 5:11

Who holds all power for ever and ever?

_____

_____

_____

_____

_____

BITE #5

With the help of Silas, whom I regard as a faithful brother, I have written to you briefly, encouraging you and testifying that this is the true grace of God. Stand fast in it.

1 Peter 5:12

Silas was a great **help** to Peter. It's been said that he wrote this letter as Peter dictated it to him. It's assumed that Silas then **delivered** the letter himself to churches of Asia Minor.

Peter calls Silas a "faithful brother." Think of three faithful girls you can depend on like sisters. List their names and write why each one is so special to you.

1._____

_____

_____

2._____

_____

_____

3._____

_____

_____

What are you doing to be a faithful sister to someone else in the body of Christ?

_____

_____

_____

_____

_____

Peter closes this verse by telling the believers to "stand fast in it." In what?

_____

_____

_____

_____

_____

She who is in Babylon, chosen together with you, sends you her greetings, and so does my son Mark.

1 Peter 5:13

"She" is the Church. Many Bible scholars will say that Babylon is a reference to **Rome**. If so, then Peter is referring to the Christians in the church in Rome. He again promotes **unity** by saying they have been "chosen together with you" and by passing along their **greetings**.

How does a greeting lift your spirits and promote unity between the sender and the receiver?

_____

_____

_____

Because we're living in such a high-tech society, letter and card writing have almost become a lost art. It's rare to receive a personal letter—a note from a friend simply to say hi. We usually get those kinds of notes through email, phone calls, or texts. Who was the last person you sent an actual letter or card to—one that required postage?

_____

_____

When was it?

_____

To whom can you send a personal greeting this week?

_____

_____

_____

Determine to **encourage** and **affirm** this person through your note or card.

Greet one another with a kiss of love. Peace to all of you who are in Christ.

1 Peter 5:14

In biblical times, greeting someone with a kiss was the common way of saying **hello**. It would be the equivalent of greeting someone with a **handshake** or a **hug** today.

How does it make you feel when someone hugs you?

_____

_____

_____

When was the last time you hugged your parents?

_____

_____

_____

Hug them today!

BITE #6

Grab a Friend

Woo-hoo! You just completed a study of the entire book of 1 Peter. How does it feel to be a Secret Power Girl who's becoming more knowledgeable about God's Word?

Now grab a friend and discuss the following questions together.

@ How have I been a servant to God's flock this week?

@ How have I shown humility this week?

@ How did I use self-control this week?

@ Whom have I encouraged this week? Whom do I need to encourage?

Memorize It!

Try to memorize this verse with your friend and say it to
each other the next time you get together:

Cast all your anxiety on him because he cares for you.

1 Peter 5:7

My Journal

Okay, Secret Power Girl, this is your space, so take
advantage of it. You can do whatever you want here, but
always try to include the following:

@ List your prayer requests. (Later, as God answers them,
go back and record the date when God answered your
prayer.)

@ Copy down any verse we studied in the previous
chapter that you don't understand. Then let this be a
reminder to ask your parents, Sunday school teacher,
pastor, or youth leader about it.

@ Jot down what stood out the most from this chapter.

@ Jot down what stood out the most from the entire
book of 1 Peter.

P.S.: (in your journal) The **title** of this book promises you'll learn how to **win**, experience **happiness**, and get a **cool wardrobe**. Because God has chosen you, you're an automatic **WINNER!** (Flip back to 1 Peter 1:2 if you need a quick refresher.) Are you **living like a winner**?

_____

_____

_____

_____

_____

Peter also explains the key to **happiness**. (Flash back to 1 Peter 2:1-3.) According to these verses, what do you need to **rid** yourself of to experience true happiness?

_____

_____

_____

_____

_____

And what about that wardrobe? A cool wardrobe is sought by many to create a beautiful outer appearance. But within a few months, as fashion changes and denim fades, the beauty vanishes with the clothes. **Your** beauty comes from a "wardrobe" that's found on the inside, one that will last forever. Reread 1 Peter 3:3-5 and jot down what comprises real beauty.

_____

_____

_____

_____

_____

Talk It Up!

Want free books?
First looks at the best new fiction?
Awesome exclusive merchandise?

We want to hear from you!

Give us your opinions on titles, covers, and stories.
Join the Z Street Team.

Email us at zstreetteam@zondervan.com
to sign up today!

Also—Friend us on Facebook!

www.facebook.com/goodteenreads

- Video Trailers
- Connect with your favorite authors
- Sneak peeks at new releases
- Giveaways
- Fun discussions
- And much more!